"Mary Morgan draws on her immense clinical experience, her warmth and her intellectual depth to explore the interplay of desire, gender, and sexuality within the ever-present tension between togetherness and separateness. She shows how early experiences shape our ability to connect, how a couple's shared unconscious phantasies, defenses, and beliefs both bind and challenge them, and how, in the context of curiosity about one another, love and hate can fuel creativity and result in mature, evolving relationships. This is a valuable resource for clinicians, scholars, and anyone seeking deeper insight into the transformative potential of love."

Harriet L. Wolfe, M.D., *International Psychoanalytical Association*

"Mary Morgan is the most important voice in the development of psychoanalytic couple psychotherapy, and in this book she takes us into new territory. With a gift for treating complex ideas with a lightness of touch whilst rendering their depth and importance, Morgan has given us the definitive introductory text. But this book is more than that. It is an invaluable guide that takes a developmental perspective on the discipline itself, tracing, remarkably succinctly, the history of analytic thinking in this area. And then, most brilliantly of all, Morgan draws links between object relations approaches, which are dominant in the UK and US, and theoretical approaches, which have grown up in France and South America. In this way, Morgan gives an unequalled international perspective on Couple Psychoanalysis. A definitive text for our times, and a perfect companion for Morgan's first book, *A Couple State of Mind: Psychoanalysis of Couples and the Tavistock Relationships Model*. Together, they are must-reads for all of us working in the field."

Andrew Balfour, Ph.D., *Chief Executive at Tavistock Relationships*

"Mary Morgan is one of the most influential exponents of the British model of psychoanalysis of couples and is a deep and effective clinician. On the basis of solid training as an individual psychoanalyst, Mary Morgan approaches the most important issues that characterise this field throughout the world and succinctly develops her findings on the mental state of the couple. This book proves to be very useful because it illustrates in an original way the historical foundations of the conjugal link with its characteristics of unity and separateness, but it also looks at the most current developments of the couple and the different forms of sexuality."

Anna Maria Nicolò, M.D., *Child Neuropsychiatrist and President of International Association for Couple and Family Psychoanalysis (IACFP)*

"A characteristic of an expert in her field is the ability convey highly complex ideas in an accessible way. In writing this book Mary Morgan has once again demonstrated her ability to do this by achieving the herculean goal of describing succinctly, yet fully and helpfully, the two major theoretical frameworks in couple and family psychoanalysis: Object Relations and Link Theory. She persuasively argues how these two approaches can be integrated and lead to a deeper understanding of the intrapsychic and interpsychic dimensions of a couple relationship. She describes how in a couple when difference can be tolerated and the power of curiosity (or the epistemophilic instinct) freed, it can facilitate the emergence of a couple state of mind. In the same way she shows how the coupling of the two main theoretical approaches can result in a new and creative approach to couple work. Moreover, in demonstrating the efficacy of her ideas with clinical cases, she also powerfully demonstrates the value of couple psychoanalysis with the contemporary problems with which couples present, especially in relation to sexual problems and issues related to sexuality. With all this achieved, I believe she highlights once again that she has become a doyen of our profession. For all these reasons, I believe this book is essential reading for all who wish to grasp the fundamentals of couple psychoanalysis or to deepen their understanding of the latest advances in the field."

Timothy Keogh, *Associate Professor, University of Sydney; Co-Chair, International Psychoanalytical Association Committee on Couple and Family Psychoanalysis (COFAP) and Former English Vice-President, International Association for Couple and Family Psychoanalysis (IACFP)*

Couple Relations

In this book, Mary Morgan provides a comprehensive understanding of couple relations.

Taking a psychoanalytic perspective, Morgan explores some of the fundamental tensions in being part of a couple: between being an individual and a couple, relating, non-relating, and the narcissistic problem in tolerating the otherness and alienness of one's partner. She guides the reader through managing feelings of both separateness and intimacy, issues around sex and sexuality, the tension between love and hate, and the importance of curiosity. She also elucidates key discoveries of unconscious processes in a couple relationship made by couple psychoanalysts, including unconscious choice of partner, the couple projective system, shared unconscious phantasy and beliefs, unconscious alliances, the couple's own transference relationship and how the real "presence" of an other is seen as an "interference" acting on the preconceptions of the other subject.

Through Morgan's accessible and holistic approach, drawing on decades of clinical experience, this book is an essential resource for all psychoanalytic and psychodynamic psychotherapists, counsellors working with couples, and researchers and students in Gender Studies, social sciences, psychology and the humanities.

Mary Morgan is a psychoanalyst, a Fellow of the British Psychoanalytic Society, a Consultant Couple Psychoanalytic Psychotherapist and a Senior Fellow of Tavistock Relationships. She is also an Honorary Member of the Polish Psychoanalytic Psychotherapy Society. She is the author of *A Couple State of Mind: Psychoanalysis of Couples and the Tavistock Relationships Model* (2019) and one of the editors of *How Couple Relationships Shape our World: Clinical Practice, Research, and Policy Perspectives* (2012).

Routledge Introductions to Contemporary Psychoanalysis

Series Editor: Aner Govrin
Executive Editor: Yael Peri Herzovich

For more information about this series, please visit: www.routledge.com/Routledge-Introductions-to-Contemporary-Psychoanalysis/book-series/ICP

Couple Relations

A Contemporary Introduction

Mary Morgan

Routledge
Taylor & Francis Group

LONDON AND NEW YORK

Designed cover image: © Michal Heiman, Asylum 1855–2020, The Sleeper (video, psychoanalytic sofa and Plate 34), exhibition view, Herzliya Museum of Contemporary Art, 2017

First published 2026
by Routledge
4 Park Square, Milton Park, Abingdon, Oxon OX14 4RN

and by Routledge
605 Third Avenue, New York, NY 10158

Routledge is an imprint of the Taylor & Francis Group, an informa business

© 2026 Mary Morgan

British Library Cataloguing-in-Publication Data
A catalogue record for this book is available from the British Library

ISBN: 978-1-032-40324-3 (hbk)
ISBN: 978-1-032-39834-1 (pbk)
ISBN: 978-1-003-35251-8 (ebk)

DOI: 10.4324/9781003352518

Typeset in Times New Roman
by Taylor & Francis Books

To Willow, Oliver, Róisín and Alice

Contents

Series Editor's Preface

Aner Govrin

Routledge Introductions to Contemporary Psychoanalysis is one of the most prominent psychoanalytic publishing ventures of our day. The series' aim is to become an encyclopedia of psychoanalysis, with each entry given its own book.

This comprehensive series illuminates the intricate landscape of psychoanalytic theory and practice. In this collection of concise yet illuminating volumes, we delve into the influential figures, groundbreaking concepts, and transformative theories that shape the contemporary psychoanalytic landscape.

At the heart of each volume lies a commitment to clarity, accessibility, and depth. Our expert authors, renowned scholars and practitioners in their respective fields, guide readers through the complexities of psychoanalytic thought with precision and enthusiasm. Whether you are a seasoned psychoanalyst, a student eager to explore the field, or a curious reader seeking insight into the human psyche, our series offers a wealth of knowledge and insight.

Each volume serves as a gateway into a specific aspect of psychoanalytic theory and practice. From the pioneering works of Sigmund Freud to the innovative contributions of modern theorists such as Antonino Ferro and Michal Eigen, our series covers a diverse range of topics, including seminal figures, key concepts, and emerging trends. Whether you are interested in classical psychoanalysis, object relations theory, or the intersection of neuroscience and psychoanalysis, you will find a wealth of resources within our collection.

One of the hallmarks of our series is its interdisciplinary approach. While rooted in psychoanalytic theory, our volumes draw upon insights from psychology, philosophy, sociology, and other disciplines to offer a holistic understanding of the human mind and its complexities.

Each volume in the series is crafted with the reader in mind, balancing scholarly rigor with engaging prose. Whether you are embarking on your journey into psychoanalysis or seeking to deepen your understanding of specific topics, our series provides a clear and comprehensive roadmap.

Moreover, our series is committed to fostering dialogue and debate within the psychoanalytic community. Each volume invites readers to critically engage with the material, encouraging reflection, discussion, and further exploration.

We invite you to join us on this journey of discovery as we explore the ever-evolving landscape of psychoanalysis.

Aner Govrin

Foreword by Francis Grier

There can be few people on the planet who know more than Mary Morgan about couple relations and couple psychoanalytic psychotherapy. She has devoted the larger part of her working life to the subject. Her knowledge comes from the ground up, in the sense that her work is grounded in the clinical experience of the consulting room. She has worked constantly with couples for 40 years, both in private practice and in one of the foremost institutional settings, Tavistock Relationships, London. She has taught generations of students – including myself – at the Tavistock, and she has travelled throughout Europe, North America, Australia and Latin America, lecturing, teaching, and supervising. She explains that in her book she will be mainly presenting couple psychotherapy as theorised by Object Relations theory and Link theory. She lives out this theory in practice through the richness of so many relationships with all manner of different objects and through the creativity of her links with them.

One of the themes of her book is the all-important quest for knowledge, Klein's epistemophilic drive and Bion's K. This theme has recently been explored and developed by Morgan's own couple partner, her husband Philip Stokoe (Stokoe, 2021), who has emphasised the centrality of curiosity, particularly curiosity about one's partner, and about one's own marriage or couple relationship. The contrast is with a narcissistic frame of mind, in which one is not genuinely curious about the idiosyncratic otherness of one's partner, since one's partner's unconscious job description is to be one's narcissistic object, not a separate person in their own right. We all have both tendencies; it's our human birthright. Conflict inevitably follows, since these two tendencies face completely opposite directions and set off opposing psychological trajectories within all couple relationships.

Curiosity about one's own mind could be described as the cornerstone of psychoanalysis itself, and Morgan, in addition to her training and practice as a couple psychotherapist, is also a fully trained and practising psychoanalyst. She is therefore fully grounded in Freud and in many psychoanalytic paradigms, which she brings to all her couple work – just as, incidentally, she brings all her couple work knowledge and experience to her psychoanalytic work with individuals. Her combination of classical psychoanalytic training with couple psychoanalytic training means that she is exceptionally able to contemplate couples as existing simultaneously on two planes, as consisting of two individual partners and also as one unit, the couple. Morgan traces how this can work out well or badly. In a benign mode, the fundamental difference and separateness of identities between the two partners keeps driving the couple unit to contain precisely this difference, which means that the container of the couple itself has to keep developing. Equally, the container of the couple as a single developmental unit keeps driving the two individuals to develop emotionally, in particular challenging their narcissism by insisting that each bears the other in mind in an attitude of concern and love deriving from the depressive position.

In a malign mode, however, the separateness and difference of the two partners can intensify and threaten to split the container, whilst the container itself can suffocate and engulf the potential creativity arising from the difference between the partners, threatening them with claustrophobic anxiety. All couples oscillate between these different positions to some extent continuously. However, normally these processes remain unconscious, certainly in the fullness and details of their operations and consequences. What is special about a theorist and practitioner of the calibre of Morgan is that she can dissect and analyse the moving components of these complex and very human dilemmas and dimensions both on a spoken level in her clinical work and in her teaching, and, as in the present case, in her writing. This enables the rest of us – whether fellow couple clinicians and authors, or interested professionals from related fields, or persons who are just very interested in couple dynamics – to gain real insight into the way this all works, both in terms of generalised theory and then focusing on particular couples. Finally, Morgan gives us the tools with which to look with renewed insight into the functioning of the various couples of which we are a part.

Morgan's own distinctive and experienced authorial voice can be heard clearly, both in her theorising and in her very lively clinical examples. But another particular feature of this book consists of her very large number of references to the literature of contemporary writers in the field. Anybody wishing to examine and read the literature on couple psychoanalytic psychotherapy from Object Relations theory, Link theory (from Latin America), and French couple and group theories will find that Morgan provides invaluable summaries from her own digesting of these vital and vitalising theories. She also gives us extremely helpful lists of references. This of course derives from Morgan's own international experience and expertise.

It will be clear from the above that Morgan is possessed of a formidable analytic intellect, but I wish to emphasise that Morgan's sharp thinking is always in a dynamic intercourse with her warm humanity. This internal coupling produces an author of truly deep empathy, which shines out from her clinical examples, as she uses her clear thinking, her sympathy and all her years of clinical experience to try to understand our very human dilemmas as we couple up with each other.

I hope that, as readers, you will benefit from reading this book as much as I have.

Reference

Stokoe, P. (2021). *The Curiosity Drive: Our Need for Inquisitive Thinking*. London: Phoenix Publishing House.

Acknowledgements

I would like to thank Willow Stokoe for her close reading of this book and the clarifying and interesting discussions that resulted. I am also very grateful to Stanley Ruszczynski and Catriona Wrottesley for reading chapters and for their helpful and insightful comments. My thanks to Elizabeth Palacios for some clarifications on the link perspective. As always, my husband Philip Stokoe has supported this project in many different ways, and I am so very grateful to him. Finally, my thanks to the many couples I have worked with over many years, to colleagues at Tavistock Relationships, past and present, and to my colleagues internationally, with whom I continue to think with and share the development of the field of couple psychoanalysis.

Introduction

A psychoanalytic approach to couple relations views unconscious processes and dynamics as central. Couple relations are a mixture of conscious and unconscious elements, as seen for example in the choice of partner. This book focuses mainly on the area of the unconscious as it exists between two people in an intimate relationship, which has been referred to as the interpsychic (Bolognini, 2010).

Intimate couple relations are a paradox. The closer one gets to an "other", the more aware one becomes of their otherness and what is not and cannot be known. But in encountering the other as other, rather than as one shaped too much by the wishes and expectations of the self, curiosity may be stimulated – leading to a wish to know the other as best as one can. This development is an authentic intimacy. In the words of James Fisher,

> Intrusive projections leave no space for the imagination. This helps us understand, I think, the fundamental difference between a genuine intimacy with the other and a 'pseudo intimacy' which is actually a narcissistic form of relating. The former is based on the fact that the reality of the other is known *only* from the outside. The latter is based on the phantasy of getting *inside* the other.
>
> (Fisher, 1999, p. 236)

The experience of an "other" seeking to know oneself is important in our early life as infants and can feel part of being authentically

DOI: 10.4324/9781003352518-1

loved as part of an adult couple. This wish to know, which Bion conceptualised as "K", also means encountering "L" (standing for love) and "H" (standing for hate). Love and hate are intrinsic parts of couple relations and can manifest in very different ways, ranging from destructive, to life giving and creative. What seems crucial is that hate is sufficiently contained by a fundamentally loving link.

The individual's biological sex, gender identification, sexual identity and sexual orientation are expressed in many ways in couple relations. These elements are formative in the way a couple conceive of their relationship, and the way they live out their sexuality within it. This can sometimes be hard to work out, not just between two different psyches but between two different bodies.

Couples are encountered in various forms along the path to becoming a part of a couple oneself. There is in us all an innate preconception of a couple or linking; there is a couple one is part of with the mother or primary carer, and later there is the awareness of the parental couple in the Oedipal situation. Within this triangular Oedipal situation, we can begin to observe ourselves as part of a couple, which may or may not come into being later in life. The capacity to be both a participant in a couple and an observer of that couple (Britton, 1998) is important once one is in an adult couple relationship of one's own and is, I believe, an important psychological development, one that I have termed a "couple state of mind" (Morgan, 2001, 2019a). Without a couple state of mind, the couple find it difficult to conceive of, and to perceive, what occurs between them. In therapeutic work with couples, the development of a couple state of mind can be considered to be an aim of the treatment.

Intimacy, otherness, love and hate, and sex and sexuality are all fundamental aspects of couple relations. These elements can be explored creatively over time in the context of a secure relationship. A less secure couple bond may lead to difficulties in facing any or all of these elements.

This book begins with an overview of the two most influential psychoanalytic approaches to couple relations. One originates in the UK, which is mainly a development of "object relations theory" in relation to a psychoanalytic understanding of, and clinical work with couples (Ruszczynski, 1993, Morgan, 2019a). It is referred to in this book as the Tavistock model or Tavistock approach, though it is not necessarily referred to in this way in other parts of the world where this perspective has also been developed.

The other approach, originating and developed primarily in South America and France, is an application of "link theory" (Berenstein, 2012) to couples (and families). It is also important to note that within the two main approaches I outline, writers emphasise different theorists or concepts and that it is a live and evolving field. There are other ways of thinking about couple relations psychoanalytically – for example, drawing on relational theory or self-psychology, which have not been written about as extensively but are elaborated in some other publications (see Nathans, 2023).

The roots of my own perspective are in the Tavistock model, having worked in Tavistock Relationships for more than 30 years and with couple relationships for over 40. During that time, I have learnt enormously from my contemporaries, and from the early pioneers of the organisation (originally called the Family Discussion Bureau). Over time I have contributed to the theory and technique of working psychoanalytically with couples. In recent years, through many international conferences and through joint publications, there has been a very fruitful exchange of ideas. I would like to acknowledge Isidoro Berenstein, the first chair of a newly created International Psychoanalytic Association Couple and Families Psychoanalysis Committee who encouraged an exchange of ideas between these different approaches (Berenstein, 2012). Other colleagues, particularly David and Jill Scharff, have been instrumental in getting papers from the link perspective translated into English, and these have enabled a more meaningful dialogue between different perspectives (Losso, de Setton & Scharff, 2018). This book is not an attempt to integrate the two approaches, and it is questionable whether an integration should be sought. Within the contemporary field, the two approaches are generally seen as complementary – some see more of the similarities and others more of the differences.

In Chapter 1, I will describe some key features of these two approaches. For the Tavistock model, I note some of the concepts that will be elaborated later in the book. For the link perspective, I have highlighted some aspects that seem particularly helpful in understanding couple relations.

In a paper in 2019, I conceptualised the theoretical stance of the Tavistock model as three domains of unconscious couple relating – the past, the present and the future (Morgan, 2019b). For me, this captured essential elements of the theoretical perspective and practice of Tavistock Relationships over the last 70 years. The past refers to the intrapsychic inner worlds of the two members of the couple that are brought to the new relationship. The present I thought of as the dynamics between the couple, especially the problem of managing difference and otherness. This might include the kind of couple they are in the present, in terms of psychic development in becoming a couple, but I would now place that in the intrapsychic domain, as it is changed by the interaction of the two partners. The future relates to what the couple newly create between them, and the potential for creative couple relating. In exploring the link perspective further for this book, it was very interesting to discover that these three areas of the couple's unconscious were presented even more clearly in several link perspectives. Thus, there is a congruence of thinking about the couple's unconscious relating as encompassing the intrapsychic, the interpersonal and the relationship as a third entity. In this important respect, the approaches of the Tavistock model and the link perspective seem to have reached a similar view of the essence of couple relations.

With that discovery, I structured Chapters 2 to 5 around these three domains. I decided that it was also important to write about sex and sexuality, as well as love, hate and creativity. Since these latter topics are so vast in themselves within psychoanalytic thinking, I chose to focus on some contemporary issues for couple relations.

Although a psychoanalytic approach to couple relations seeks to understand the couple relationship – what occurs in the "in between" of the pair – a couple is also made up of two individuals. Therefore, it seems important to address the psychic development that occurs in the individual partners in terms of how it enables or impairs their capacity to form a couple. From the Tavistock approach comes the idea of the adult couple relationship potentially fostering the continuous psychic development of each partner within it, and alternatively how a relationship can also be sacrificed to maintain the psychic equilibrium of each partner. Thus, in Chapter 2 I look at the intrapsychic, in particular the psychic developments that occur in potentially becoming a couple.

In Chapter 3, the concept of projective identification (Klein, 1946, 1952) is explored. This has been central in the object relations approach to the couple, especially the way in which it is manifest between the couple in what is understood as a projective system. Different kinds of projective identification lead to different forms of projective systems in a couple, from the more containing, flexible and communicative, to the more rigid, intrusive and defensive. In the unconscious choice of partner, these different forms of projective identification come into play along with transference, which may stimulate the need to repeat or resolve earlier object relationships. Concepts from the link perspective of "interference" and "uncertainty" provide a helpful counterpoint to these ideas (Puget, 2010, Berenstein, 2012).

Shared unconscious phantasy and unconscious beliefs in a couple relationship are managed by the creation of shared defences. While the phantasies and beliefs may be hard to access, the way these become manifest in the couple's structuring of their relationship is more apparent. I have suggested that the defensive form of Käes' concept of unconscious alliances, which is a key concept in the French link perspective, might resonate with this idea of shared beliefs and shared defences (Käes, 2019). Undoing the shared defences aimed at keeping unconscious beliefs out of mind requires the activation of curiosity (Stokoe, 2021). These concepts are the areas discussed in Chapter 4.

In Chapter 5, a fundamental issue in couple relations, that of intimacy and otherness, is addressed. The otherness of the other, also conceptualised as "alienness", has been compellingly described from the link perspective. Many couple relationships struggle in this area of togetherness and separateness – if the otherness of the other cannot be tolerated, the couple may form various kinds of narcissistic pacts; for example, one of merger, or intrusiveness or sado-masochism. The dynamic interplay between relating and non-relating, or narcissism and the psychological state of "marriage", is also considered – i.e., the idea that in couple relations there is an oscillation between these different psychological states.

Having looked at the first two domains of intrapsychic and interpersonal, in Chapter 6 I explore the relationship as a "third". This is the idea that the relationship (which is jointly created by the two members of the couple) is a psychic entity in itself that can function in different ways. Here I start with the link perspective because the "third" that is inevitably created in a relationship between two or more is the link itself. The link is a new entity, which is not simply the aggregate of the two psyches. The link, once created, influences and shapes the couple.

The idea of a third, co-created entity that then influences the members of the couple has been described in several other ways – for example, through the concept of shared unconscious phantasy and beliefs (Bannister & Pincus, 1965, Britton, 1998, Morgan, 2010), through a projective system as in a "joint marital personality" (Dicks, 1967/1993), or a couple ego and couple superego (Kernberg, 1993). Other kinds of thirds seen within the Tavistock approach function in a relationship as a symbolic entity and arise from psychic developments occurring within the couple – fostering containment (Colman, 1993), reflective space (Ruszczynski, 2005) and creativity (Morgan, 2005).

Sex and sexuality are the focus of Chapter 7. I explore several areas that seem especially relevant to contemporary couple relations. Sexual desire and the loss of desire is considered from different theoretical viewpoints. As same sex relationships become more commonplace, one can see the disturbing impact of internalised homophobia on some couples. The structuring of couple relations beyond monogamy is a contemporary issue, as different forms of coupling are being explored by some. The impact of social media and pornography on psychosexual development is of concern especially in relation to young people.

In Chapter 8, I look at love, hate and creativity in couple relationships. Love has generally been conceptualised in psychoanalysis, and within other fields, as one of an initial in-love state that gradually gives way to a mature love. Some couples find this transition very difficult, and I reflect on some of the reasons why this might be. I also consider the view that illusion, regression and unintegrated states, usually associated with the in-love state, might also have an important role in mature love. Aggression is usually thought of as part of the life force interacting with love. Hate can be more problematic, manifesting destructively in violent relationships. However, love and hate can be contained within a secure enough relationship, and in being so can lead to creative developments in the couple.

Couple relationships are central in our psyches. The presence of an internal creative couple is important in our engagement with many realms of life – in our sexual relations, in our coupling, in our parenting, in whatever forms these take. It affects the way we engage with others and the world around us. I hope this book will provide a useful introduction to the unconscious world of couple relations from a psychoanalytic perspective.

References

Bannister, K. & Pincus, L. (1965). *Shared Phantasy in Marital Problems: Therapy in a Four-Person Relationship*. London: Institute of Marital Studies.

Berenstein, I. (2012). Vínculo as a relationship between others. *Psychoanalytic Quarterly*, 81 (3): 565–577.

Bolognini, S. (2010). *Secret Passages: Theory and Technique of the Interpsychic Dimension*. London: Routledge.

Britton, R. (1998). Belief and psychic reality. In: R. Britton, *Belief and Imagination: Explorations in Psychoanalysis* (pp. 8–18). London: Routledge.

Colman, W. (1993). Marriage as a psychological container. In: S. Ruszczynski (Ed.), *Psychotherapy with Couples: Theory and Practice at the Tavistock Institute of Marital Studies* (pp. 70–96). London: Karnac.

Dicks, H. V. (1967/1993). *Marital Tensions: Clinical Studies towards a Psychological Theory of Interaction*. London: Karnac.

Fisher, J. (1999). *The Uninvited Guest: Emerging from Narcissism towards Marriage*. London: Karnac.

Käes, R. (2019). *Linking, Alliances, and Shared Space: Groups and the Psychoanalyst*. London: Routledge.

Kernberg, O. F. (1993). The couple's constructive and destructive superego functions. *Journal of the American Psychoanalytic Association*, 41 (3): 653–677.

Klein, M. (1946). Notes on some schizoid mechanisms. *International Journal of Psycho-Analysis*, 27: 99–110.

Klein, M. (1952). Notes on some schizoid mechanisms. In: M. Klein, P. Heimann, S. Isaacs & J. Riviere (Eds.), *Developments in Psycho-Analysis* (pp. 292–320). London: Hogarth Press.

Losso, R., de Setton, L., & Scharff, D. (Eds.) (2018). *The Linked Self in Psychoanalysis: The Pioneering Work of Enrique Pichon Riviere.* London: Karnac.

Morgan, M. (2001). First contacts: The therapist's "couple state of mind" as a factor in the containment of couples seen for initial consultations. In: F. Grier (Ed.), *Brief Encounters with Couples* (pp. 17–32). London: Karnac.

Morgan, M. (2005). On being able to be a couple: The importance of a "creative couple" in psychic life. In: F. Grier (Ed.), *Oedipus and the Couple* (pp. 9–30). London: Karnac.

Morgan, M. (2010). Unconscious beliefs about being a couple. *Fort Da,* 16 (1): 36–55.

Morgan, M. (2019a). Love, hate, and otherness in intimate relating. *Couple and Family Psychoanalysis,* 9: 15–21.

Morgan, M. (2019b). *A Couple State of Mind: Psychoanalysis of Couples and the Tavistock Relationships Model.* London & New York: Routledge.

Nathans, S. (Ed.) (2023). *More about Couples on the Couch: Approaching Psychoanalytic Couple Psychotherapy from an Expanded Perspective.* London & New York: Routledge.

Puget, J. (2010). The subjectivity of certainty and the subjectivity of uncertainty. *Psychoanalytic Dialogues,* 20 (1): 4–20.

Ruszczynski, S. (Ed.) (1993). *Psychotherapy with Couples: Theory and Practice at the Tavistock Institute of Marital Studies.* London: Karnac.

Ruszczynski, S. (2005). Reflective space in the intimate couple relationship: The marital triangle. In: F. Grier (Ed.), *Oedipus and the Couple* (pp. 31–47). London: Karnac.

Stokoe, P. (2021). *The Curiosity Drive: Our Need for Inquisitive Thinking.* London: Phoenix Publishing House.

Chapter 1

An overview of the field

A psychoanalytic understanding of couple relations may seem relatively new and even unknown to some in the wider psychoanalytic field. However, it is not that new. It was in the 1940s, in the UK and in Argentina, that psychoanalytic thinking about couple relations began to evolve.

The origins of the two main approaches within the field of couple relations stemmed from very different cultural, political and psychoanalytic traditions within the UK and Argentina. In the UK, Tavistock Relationships (originally the Family Discussion Bureau) was established by Enid Eichholtz (later Enid Balint) and colleagues.* This was a state-sponsored organisation which aimed to help families torn apart by WW2. At the same time, Henry Dicks created the Marital Unit at the Tavistock Clinic, which was part of the National Health Service. The two organisations exchanged ideas and were, as Dicks describes, "the best of rivals with usefully complementary roles, and some overlap of staff" (Dicks, 1967/1993, p. xix.). Between them they developed an expanded object relations approach to understanding the couple relationship. This was the beginning of the "Tavistock model" of couple psychoanalysis. The 1960s heralded the first publications from these bodies; Lily Pincus wrote *Marriage: Studies in Emotional Conflict and Growth* (1960) and Dicks wrote his ground-breaking *Marital Tensions: Clinical Studies Towards a Psychological Theory of Interaction* (1967).

This object relations approach has been influential in many parts of Europe, the United States, Australia, China and Russia

DOI: 10.4324/9781003352518-2

and other parts of the world. Some of the main disseminators of the approach – for example, David Scharff and Jill Savege Scharff in the USA and Charles Enfield in Australia – had all studied and worked at the Tavistock Clinic and drew on object relations thinking – developing and conceptualising it in slightly different ways. Tavistock Relationships disseminated this approach particularly in Northern Europe, San Francisco, Washington and New York. In most recent years, Stanley Ruszczynski and Mary Morgan have conducted trainings in three different regions in Poland (see Dembińska-Krajewska et al., 2021). As key texts from this approach are translated into other languages, this psychoanalytic approach to couples (and families) continues to develop in other parts of the world.

Another approach, the link perspective, originated in the innovative work of Enrique Pichon Rivière in the Río de la Plata region (concentrated around the cities of Buenos Aires and Montevideo) and was applied to couple relations from the 1960s in Argentina before expanding throughout Latin America and parts of Europe. As with object relations theory, the link perspective is an entire psychoanalytic approach which has been elaborated on by those analysts interested in understanding couples (and families). In France, the link perspective was also developed by René Käes. Käes had a close relationship with psychoanalysts from the Río de La Plata region and was interested in the metapsychology of links, thought of as a "third metapsychology".

The link perspective has developed in somewhat different ways in different countries. It is the main couple and family psychoanalytic approach in Latin America. Isidoro Berenstein and Janine Puget, amongst others, were very influential in developing the link perspective in relation to couples in South America. In Spain, France and Italy, the Latin American link perspective, along with the work of Käes, is particularly influential.

Object relations theory and the Tavistock model

Object relation theory mainly refers to the work of Ronald Fairbairn, Donald Winnicott and Michael Balint but often also includes Melanie Klein and Wilfred Bion among others. It is contrasted with Freud's focus on instinctual impulses and drive theory, and as Fairbairn emphasised, the individual is seen as not pleasure-seeking but object-seeking. Object in this sense means the person towards whom one's feelings and needs are expressed from the beginning of life. It is often described as a move from the idea of a "one-person" psychology (Freud) to that of a "two-person" psychology. The relationship involves not only the way the subject perceives his objects but the way the object shapes the subject.

An internal world of (object) relationships is envisaged which interacts with the external world. The internal world provides a lens shaping one's perception of the external world. New experiences from the external world can modify the internal lens, thus there is a dynamic interplay between the psychic reality of the internal world and the reality of the external.

At the beginning, the clinicians at Tavistock Relationships turned to established psychoanalytic thinking to understand the unconscious dynamics in couple relations. Concepts that were rooted in the intrapsychic world of an individual, such as unconscious phantasy or projective identification, were applied to the couple relationship as "shared unconscious phantasy" and as a "couple projective system". Kathleen Bannister and Lily Pincus, early clinicians at Tavistock Relationships, became aware of the complexity of couple relations.

> When dealing with a disturbed marriage, both the individuals and the relationship between them must be the object of study. We have to be aware that each is both subject and object. Each is a subject in his own right, but has taken the other, in some measure, as his object and is also the object of the other's attachment. There is a complicated interaction going on between the two, a mutual psycho-biological system in which the adaptive and defensive processes of each are geared in with those of the other and have to function in relation to the other.
>
> (Bannister & Pincus, 1965, p. 61)

More recent couple analytic concepts have included what the couple create together, particularly the idea of the "creative couple" (Morgan, 2005). In a creative couple process the members of the couple can "tolerate differences, not necessarily knowing if and how these differences can be brought together, but nonetheless hold the belief, sometimes realised, that their differences can lead to a creative outcome, something 'new' between them that neither could have discovered alone" (Morgan, 2019, p. xxiv). Thus, there is both subject-to-object and subject-to-subject relations. However, it is important to point out that the latter is foundational to the link perspective and is often contrasted with the early couple object relations perspective in this way.

The Tavistock approach is considered within the wider field of analytic couple relations thinking as an object relations approach. This is true in many ways, and Dicks in particular began his theorising by turning to Fairbairn, though he also drew on the work of Klein. In Tavistock Relationships, while the influence of object relations thinking is strong, it does in fact draw on quite a wide group of analytic thinkers. At the beginning, there were several key Jungian thinkers, and though less present now, some of the ideas from this perspective are still embedded in the overall approach. For example, the idea of "individuation" is a Jungian concept that contributed to the understanding of an adult couple relationship as being potentially developmental and therefore therapeutic. Attachment theory has also been extensively explored in relation to couple interaction and integrated into some of the thinking. Klein's concepts of the paranoid-schizoid and depressive position have been important concepts in helping to understand unconscious couple interaction and the nature of couple relating, from the more primitive dynamics, to the more mature. Her concept of projective identification was essential for both Dick's formulation of the "joint marital personality" (Dicks, 1967/1993) as well as the Tavistock Relationships development of it as a "couple projective system" and an "unconscious choice of partner" (Pincus, 1962).

Post-Kleinian thinking has been influential, since many concepts developed within that school lend themselves to an understanding of couple relations. For example, Britton's concept of a "third position", which along with the Tavistock Relationships thinking of the "couple as patient" came together in the formulation of the concept of a "couple state of mind" (Britton, 1989, Morgan, 2001, 2019). These post-Kleinian ideas have been usefully contrasted with Winnicottian thinking; for example, the idea of "gesture and recognition" between a couple as an alternative to projective identification (Colman, 1995). More recently, other writers have further explored Winnicott's thinking to provide another lens on couple relations (Joyce, 2019, Friend, 2021, Hewison, 2023).

Several concepts have developed within this approach which are summarised here and referred to later in this book:

- Unconscious choice of partner and couple fit;
- A couple projective system, constructed developmentally or defensively with a dynamic tension between these two aspects;
- A joint marital personality and unconscious complementariness;
- Narcissistic relating versus a capacity for managing separateness, difference and otherness;
- Shared unconscious phantasy and unconscious beliefs about being a couple;
- The transference relationship between the couple;
- The relationship as a psychological container;
- The marital triangle;
- A couple state of mind and the creative couple.

The link perspective

Roberto Losso, Lea de Setton and David Scharff, among others, have been instrumental in bringing the work of Pichon Rivière into the awareness of English-speaking couple and family psychoanalysis (Losso, de Setton, & Scharff, 2017).

Scharff and Savege Scharff introduce the concept of the link in the following way:

Each person is born into links and lives in links. Through the link, what is interactive or interpersonal becomes intrapsychic, and what is intrapsychic becomes interpersonal, or, to use a more recent term, interpsychic (Bolognini, 2010). The concept of the link emphasizes that the ongoing bond between two people is built by their interaction, while at the same time it influences the internal world of each of them ... One pattern of organisation joins with other organisational patterns to produce a new, overarching higher-level pattern that could not be predicted from knowledge of the interacting components that produce it.

(Scharff & Savege Scharff, 2011, p. 27)

In the following, I will summarise some of the key aspects of the link perspective that seem especially useful in understanding couple relations. This is not in any way a comprehensive account of the link perspective as a whole. For further reading on the link perspective and couple relations in the English language, I would recommend Berenstein (2012) and the articles in Volume 6 (2) of *Couple and Family Psychoanalysis* (Karnac).

Links are emotional bonds between the self and other that continue throughout life. Each person is born into and shaped by links. There are two axes of the link, one vertical and one horizontal. The vertical axis links each person to their cultural and historical roots, including previous generations. The horizontal axis links each person to their couple, family, community and wider society.

Once constructed, the links that one is born into and are part of creating oneself function as a third entity which then also influences the members of the link. The individuals forming a couple, through their meeting, unconsciously create a new link specific to them. It may be constructed with different kinds of "unconscious alliances" (Käes, 2016), some positively expressing themes for the couple, others that are more defensive.

Anna Maria Nicolò emphasises that the link is not something we can see directly but is revealed in the way it affects the freedom of expression of the members of the link. It is unconscious, "usually located in the background, just like a set on stage is usually not dominant [...] while the actors play the different parts of the play" (Nicolò, 2016, p. 210).

Pichon Rivière saw the internal and external world meeting together in the link and continually interacting and shaping each other. This is a different emphasis from object relations theory, which is more focussed on the internal world of the subject and its relations to the object, in phantasy or reality. However, in the development of a *couple* object relations approach, inevitably an emphasis has been given to the impact on each partner of the real other – i.e., not only the other as perceived in unconscious phantasy.

In a couple or a family, different members of the group may express different aspects of their shared link. This might mean that a particular member is seen as the patient or "symptom bearer" (Käes, 2019), but this "weaker" member may in fact be the stronger member in that he or she is able to carry something on behalf of the other(s). A similar concept, developed by Pichon Rivière, is that of the "spokesperson", who presents as the most psychologically disturbed member of the group and acts as an informer through dreaming, symptom formation, speaking and behaviour for what is going on in the group's dynamics.

The link that the couple form is not simply an aggregate of their two internal worlds (of links) but a newly formed entity, which neither could predict or form without the other and which is continuously being created. Berenstein captures the essence of this in the following description of the link in couple relations:

> This model is based on the notion of vínculo as an exchange between two or more. Its product is an expanded, modified, renewed subjectivity that makes it possible to negate the ego's (narcissistic) confinement in its identity and to establish this subjectivity as novelty. The couple has its own life as an aggregate, which is different from the sum of its parts. Its members carry in them the psychic developments of their own history and childhood as well as those produced within this aggregate, which is ceaselessly being constituted in each of the numerous 'nows' they experience together. The present time gives rise to a past, a history, and a future in the form of a project that may not necessarily be realized but is a determining factor nonetheless.
>
> (Berenstein, 2012, p. 573)

In the link, the "presence" of the other acts as an "interference" on the subjectivity of the self. This means that the encounter with the other in a relationship affects the individual's own pre-conceptions, making it impossible to remain who they were before, though each partner may resist this interference. It is further argued that there is a part of the other that can never be known or identified with by the subject. This is the "otherness of the other", an idea developed particularly by Berenstein and Puget. Berenstein states that,

> Notwithstanding identification, something of the other resists and cannot be incorporated; indeed, even in the similar and the different there is a part of the other that cannot be inscribed as the subject's own, and which remains unknown—namely the alien, which is inherent in the presence of the other.
>
> (2001, p. 145)

Puget also introduces the idea of "uncertainty", which is always present in the link and is in tension with the couple's wish for the familiar (Puget, 2010). These dynamics cause what has been described as "suffering in the link". "Suffering in the link is a concept that tries to describe the psychic pain, distress, or affliction that results from being part of shared links in couples or families" (Palacios & Monserrat, 2017, pp. 65–66).

Some differences and similarities

An exploration of the relationship between these different psychoanalytic approaches has to some extent been hampered by the lack of translation of publications, which, though changing, remains an issue, meaning that many couple and family analysts have only a partial view of the entire field. The International Psychoanalytic Association's Committee on Couple and Family Psychoanalysis (COFAP) and the International Association for Couple and Family Psychoanalysis (IACFP) have collaborated in articulating and sharing these different approaches through conferences and publications so that in recent years there has been increasingly informative and meaningful dialogue.

One of the main differences between these two approaches is articulated by Nicolò:

> The link differs from the object relationship (Berenstein & Puget, 1997) because it is a third-party construction as compared with the subjects who produce it. Instead, the object relationship, even though it produces 'a shared object' (Teruel, 1966) in the exchange, and even though it is at the base of a couple's collusion and fruit of projection, and reciprocal projective identification, it is the re-updating of an internal object relationship that has its origins in the past.
>
> (Nicolò, 2016, p. 210)

This description highlights the difference between a couple interaction that repeats aspects of the past, albeit in a current version, and a couple interaction that creates something new in the present. Both processes occur in couple relations and so perhaps each of the two approaches emphasises one side of this duality.

The interaction between two psyches in couple relations can thus be thought about from different vantage points – from the inside out and from the outside in. The inside out encompasses ideas about how the internal world of each partner, the intrapsychic, affects each person's perception and experience of the other, how each subject relates to the other as both object and subject. The Tavistock approach began with the internal world of each partner and how these internal object relations manifested and were responded to by the other in the couple relationship.

The outside in encompasses how the real "presence" of an other affects each partner as a subject. From the beginning Pichon Rivière gave much more prominence to the continuously interacting role of the external world – the social and the cultural – with the internal world of the subject, each influencing the other. However, as described above, the internal world and the intrapsychic of each subject is also a central part of the link perspective, and object relations thinking developed within the couple relations field to understand what happens in the dynamics between the two subjects. Both these perspectives, unlike the classical Freudian approach, are two-person psychologies.

The approaches are often juxtaposed to each other, as their starting point or logic is different. Indeed, the link perspective has a very different starting point from Freud's original metapsychology. However, across the field of couple psychoanalysis, these perspectives are usually seen as complementary in making important contributions to understanding couple relations. A synthesis of the Tavistock model and the link perspective is not the aim of this introduction to couple relations, even if that were possible to achieve. This book will be grounded in the Tavistock model but also draw on some of the important and illuminating concepts from the link perspective.

The detailed history of the development of these schools of thought has been well documented elsewhere and will not be repeated here. Fuller elaborations of the Tavistock model and the link perspectives history and development of ideas can be found in Balfour (2021), Ruszczynski (1993) and in Scharff and Palacios (2017).

The three domains of couple relations

It is interesting that these approaches all conclude that there are three fundamental interrelating dimensions of couple relations. Morgan has described the Tavistock model as consisting of the influence of the past, present and future on the couple relationship (Morgan, 2016). Simply put, the past refers to the intrapsychic and that which each partner brings to the couple relationship of their early experience and internal world and how this is lived out in different ways within the relationship. The present focuses on the dynamics between the couple in the present – including the problem of managing difference and otherness as part of intimacy. The future addresses that which the couple create newly together and how this shapes the relationship – the relationship becoming a third object for each partner. Judith Pickering, from an object relations/Jungian perspective, describes these three dimensions of couple relations in the following way:

> There are the two partners, the complex networks, and dynamics of relations between them and the relationship itself, which creates a fluid, interpenetrating and interacting field, the

intersubjective marital third. This is revealed by the communication of the individuals but controlled by neither.

(Pickering, 2008, p. 10)

From a broader theoretical psychoanalytic perspective (i.e., not only referring to couples and families but to any relationship of one or more), René Käes describes the French link perspective as the relationship between three interfering spaces, proposing the hypothesis:

that in groups there exists not only one psychic space, being that of the group, but three. The first space is that of the 'individual subject'. The second is that of 'intersubjective links' that subjects develop when encountering an other or more than one other, whether in the group, the couple, the family or in institutions. The third is that of 'the ensemble' which they build, and which they constitute while it constitutes them.

(Käes, 2016, p. 183)

Elizabeth Palacios refers to Berenstein's and Puget's conceptualisation and also picks up on these three dimensions:

They suggested three psychic spaces across each subjectivity: an intrasubjective space that has to do with drives and phantasy; the intersubjective space where two or more subjects meet; and a trans-subjective space where subjects participate in a specific culture and are part of a society that gives a sense of belonging.

(Palacios, 2017, p. 9)

This is similar to other formulations except that the trans-subjective space is a third that importantly places the couple within the societal context.

Integrating these perspectives into a psychoanalytic understanding of couple relations, Nicolò argues that,

We really must then see three levels: an intra-psychic functioning, a second level represented by the different object relationships that lie between that subject and the object of his/her projection, and a third level that we can call the link, one that lies between two or more subjects and that is characteristic of the relationship between a subject and another subject.

(Nicolò, 2016, p. 212)

These different approaches, developed in different parts of the world, and within different psychoanalytic frameworks, have not until quite recently come into contact with one another sufficiently, partly to do with the barrier of language. Just as in couple relations differences are important to acknowledge and can potentially be creative, so too here. Nonetheless, both approaches (and the differences within each of them) seem to conclude that a psychoanalytic understanding of couple relations needs to encompass these three domains.

The chapters that follow elaborate key concepts that can be thought of as *within* these domains, even though they inevitably overlap with others.

1   The individual in couple relations and the process of psychic development for each partner in becoming part of a couple and how this will impact on the relationship the couple form.
2   The interpersonal and the interpsychic (Bolognini, 2010) dynamics between the members of a couple.
3   What the couple co-create and the different conceptualisations of the relationship as a third.

In the last two chapters, two other fundamental aspects of couple relations will be explored – sex and sexuality, and love, hate and creativity.

Note

* The Family Discussion Bureau changed its name several times as will be seen in publications over the years. It later became the Institute of Marital Studies, the Tavistock Institute of Marital studies, the Tavistock Marital Studies Institute, the Tavistock Centre for Couple Relationships and is currently known as Tavistock Relationships.

References

Balfour, A. (2021). A brief history of Tavistock Relationships. In: M. Waddell & S. Kraemer (Eds.), *The Tavistock Century 2020 Vision* (pp. 17–181). London: Phoenix.

Bannister, K. & Pincus, L. (1965). *Shared Phantasy in Marital Problems: Therapy in a Four-Person Relationship*. London: Institute of Marital Studies.

Berenstein, I. (2001). The link and the other. *International Journal of Psycho-Analysis*, 82: 141–149.

Berenstein, I. (2012). Vínculo as a relationship between others. *Psychoanalytic Quarterly*, 81 (3): 565–577.

Bolognini, S. (2010). *Secret Passages: Theory and Technique of the Interpsychic Dimension*. London: Routledge.

Britton, R. (1989). The missing link: Parental sexuality in the Oedipus Complex. In: J. Steiner (Ed.), *The Oedipus Complex Today: Clinical Implications* (pp. 83–101). London: Karnac.

Colman, W. (1995). Gesture and recognition: An alternative model to projective identification as a basis for couple relationships. In: S. Ruszczynski & J. V. Fisher (Eds.), *Intrusiveness and Intimacy in the Couple* (pp. 59–73). London: Karnac.

Dembińska-Krajewska, D., Prot-Klinger, K., Kalita, L. & Groth, J. (2021). Enduring the chaos: Psychoanalytical psychotherapy in Poland. *Psychoanalytic Psychotherapy*, 35 (2): 124–140.

Dicks, H. V. (1967/1993). *Marital Tensions: Clinical Studies towards a Psychological Theory of Interaction*. London: Karnac.

Friend, J. (2021). Creative illusion in couples: Thoughts about the value of transitional experience for couple relationships. *Couple and Family Psychoanalysis*, 11 (2): 158–169.

Hewison, D. (2023). Re-visioning creativity in couple psychanalysis: The importance of Winnicott and Bollas in clinical practice. In: S. Nathans (Ed.), *More about Couples on the Couch: Approaching Psychoanalytic Couple Psychotherapy from an Expanded Perspective*. London & New York: Routledge.

Joyce, A. (2019). The couple, the self, and the problem of the other. *Couple and Family Psychoanalysis*, 6 (2): 154–166.

Käes, R. (2016). Link and transference within three interfering spaces. *Couple and Family Psychoanalysis*, 6 (2): 181–193.

Käes, R. (2019). *Linking, Alliances, and Shared Space: Groups and the Psychoanalyst*. London: Routledge.

Losso, R., de Setton, L., & Scharff, D. (Eds.) (2017). *The Linked Self in Psychoanalysis: The Pioneering Work of Enrique Pichon Riviere.* London: Karnac.

Morgan, M. (2001). First contacts: The therapist's "couple state of mind" as a factor in the containment of couples seen for initial consultations. In: F. Grier (Ed.), *Brief Encounters with Couples* (pp. 17–32). London: Karnac.

Morgan, M. (2005). On being able to be a couple: The importance of a "creative couple" in psychic life. In: F. Grier (Ed.), *Oedipus and the Couple* (pp. 9–30). London: Karnac.

Morgan, M. (2016). An Object Relations approach to the couple relationship: Past, present and future. *Couple and Family Psychoanalysis*, 6 (2): 194–205.

Morgan, M. (2019). *A Couple State of Mind: Psychoanalysis of Couples and the Tavistock Relationships Model.* London & New York: Routledge.

Nicolò, A. M. (2016). Thinking in terms of links. *Couple and Family Psychoanalysis*, 6 (2): 206–214.

Palacios, E. (2017). An Argentine approach to family therapy. In: D. E. Scharff & E. Palacios (Eds.), *Family and Couple Psychoanalysis: A Global Perspective.* London: Karnac.

Palacios, E. & Monserrat, A. (2017). Contributions to the link perspective in interventions with families: Theoretical and technical aspects, and clinical application. In: D. E. Scharff & E. Palacios (Eds.), *Family and Couple Psychoanalysis: A Global Perspective.* London: Karnac.

Pickering, J. (2008). *Being in Love: Therapeutic Pathways through Psychological Obstacles to Love.* London & New York: Routledge.

Pincus, L. (1962). The nature of marital interaction. In: Institute of Marital Studies (Ed.), *The Marital Relationship as a Focus for Casework* (pp. 13–25). London: Institute of Marital Studies.

Puget, J. (2010). The subjectivity of certainty and the subjectivity of uncertainty. *Psychoanalytic Dialogues*, 20 (1): 4–20.

Ruszczynski, S. (1993). Theory and practice of the Tavistock Institute of Marital Studies. In: S. Ruszczynski (Ed.), *Psychotherapy with Couples: Theory and Practice at the Tavistock Institute of Marital Studies* (pp. 3–23). London: Karnac.

Scharff, D. E. & Palacios, E. (Eds.) (2017). *Family and Couple Psychoanalysis: A Global Perspective.* London: Karnac.

Scharff, D. E. & Savege Scharff, J. (2011). *The Interpersonal Unconscious.* Northvale, NJ: Jason Aronson.

Chapter 2

The intrapsychic and the individual within a relationship

Although the main focus of a contemporary analytic understanding of couple relations is on the dynamics between the two members of the couple and the relationship they co-create, there is also, at the same time, two individuals within a relationship, and sometimes more than two in the case of polyamory, some forms of open relationships, and other conceptions of intimate adult relating.

The psychic development of each individual and their respective inner world affects the relationship(s) the couple later form. Early experience and subsequent lived history, including what may be carried dormant in the psyche transgenerationally, and different sociocultural experiences all have an influence. All these aspects impact the way each partner sees the world and relates to others. Once part of a couple, the two worlds of the individuals meet. The interpersonal relationship impacts on and changes the intrapsychic world of each partner within it in unpredictable ways. As Thomas Ogden describes, the alterity of the other affects our sense of who we are and "does not allow us to remain who we were" (1994, p. 14).

Alongside the unconscious and unpredictable interactions of each partner's psyche affecting each of them in the present, the relationship may be used to work through or defend against unresolved experiences in the past. The early clinicians in the Tavistock approach hypothesised that in each partner there is an unconscious recognition of some parts of the self, represented in the other via projective processes. This could be seen as part of their unconscious choice of partner, occurring alongside a conscious choice. Within the safety and intimacy of an adult couple

DOI: 10.4324/9781003352518-3

relationship (and sometimes with the containment of a therapeutic process) it is possible for these split off aspects to be worked through and over time to be reintegrated into the self. Unexpected primitive feelings from earlier in life can also be stirred up; for example, anxieties about dependency or abandonment, and if the couple feel secure in their coupling, they may feel supported by the relationship to be able to approach these again. Thus, once part of a couple, psychic development and growth can continue for each partner through the experience of being part of a couple.

What is newly imposed on the self through being in a relationship – the other's "presence" – also acts as an "interference" (Berenstein, Katz & Filc, 2012) on the self and must also be dealt with. Whether stemming from the inside, the intrapsychic, or from the outside, due to the encounter with an "other", this can be a developmental process or a defensive one.

The relationship can also be used defensively to deal with unmetabolised or unwanted parts of the self by projecting them into the other and, through unconscious forms of relating, find ways of keeping them in the other. In that situation, as John Zinner describes, "the quality of the marital relationship is sacrificed to the need to minimise inner tension within the individual partner" (Zinner, 1988, p. 2).

The couple projective system and developmental and defensive choice of partner will be discussed more fully in Chapter 3. The relevance of those ideas here is that the psychic development of the individual shapes couple relations later in life, and the couple relationship that is formed can enable or resist psychic development in the individual members of the couple. In the remainder of this chapter, I will suggest some of the key psychic developments in the individual that contribute to the process of forming a couple. Where these developments have been curtailed or problematic they may also create difficulties once being part of a couple.

Psychic development in becoming a couple

The individual's psychic growth and development occurs in conjunction with, and is stimulated by, physiological growth and the response of the environment. Whether or not an actual couple relationship is formed, these developments also mean that an internal capacity for relating to another develops. This capacity impacts upon all forms of relating; for example, with friends, family, colleagues and with the world around oneself, not just within intimate couple relations.

For many there is a natural trajectory towards becoming part of a couple. For everyone, forming a relationship is an internal process as well as an external one and can be seen as part of their respective psychic development. Many individuals strive to be part of an intimate couple, but achieving this may take many attempts. Working out what kind of couple relationship one wants to be part of can take time and may not be a straightforward process. Once part of a couple, the relationship may, for some, be difficult to sustain.

During psychic development, there are different versions of couples, couple relating and relationships that are encountered and which all affect the individual's conception of what a couple is or could be. These experiences contribute to later being able to imagine oneself as part of a couple. New and unpredictable developments occur when part of a couple and through the life cycle of the couple. Sometimes the relationship functions to contain these elements and consequently the individual and the relationship is strengthened. For others, these changes and challenges threaten the core of the relationship.

Three of the areas of psychic development that contribute to the capacity for adult intimate coupling or internal relating are 1) the first relationship with the primary object or caregiver; 2) the early Oedipal situation; and 3) adolescence. These "stages" are not as linear as they will appear in the following account, because the experiences and demands at these points of development are returned to at other points as they are encountered again in different ways and from different positions. Being part of a couple can stimulate primitive regressions, and many anxieties – for example, about dependence, separateness, togetherness, inclusion and exclusion – as these are revisited.

The first relationship

Psychic development from the beginning of life occurs within the context of relationships to key figures. Much attention, rightly so, has been given by psychoanalysts to the first relationship, the bond between the primary caregiver and the infant. It is no ordinary bond but one in which the psychological growth of the infant begins. Winnicott believed there was a process of natural development that occurred if the infant was provided with "holding" (Winnicott, 1965). The mother or primary carer mediates the infant's gradual adaptation to reality by the provision of a facilitating environment, which ensures the infant's continuity of being.

Bion thought about early development in a different way. This was formulated in his concept of containment. Here the mother or primary carer processes the infant's unmetabolised and anxious states, through taking them inside herself and using her "reverie", to make sense of them. Once transformed by the mother's reverie, the previously unmetabolised states can potentially be taken back by the infant in a more digestible form. Bion called these unprocessed states "beta elements", and the processed states "alpha elements". The mother's/primary carer's capacity to transform beta elements into alpha elements he called "alpha function". Eventually, this capacity for "alpha function" is itself introjected by the infant, who is gradually able to process his own emotional states and psychologically grow (Bion, 1962, 1963).

These two models, described only very briefly here, probably occur together in good enough mothering and parenting. It is also important to note that these are processes that often occur naturally in the mother/primary carer and infant relationship and provide a good foundation for the developing self. However, too much of a failure in holding or containment can create difficulties later; for example, in being able to feel a secure sense of "going-on-being", in being able to process and manage one's own and others' emotional states, and in being able to be creative.

Other psychoanalytic thinkers have argued that there is an innate or inborn preconception of a couple in each of us, something unconsciously waiting to be met with through the actual experience of being part of a couple, initially with the primary carer. Roger Money-Kyrle formulated the idea of an innate preconception as follows:

[A]n innate preconception, then, if it exists, is something we use without being able to imagine it. I think of it as having some of the qualities of a forgotten word. Various words suggest themselves to us, which we have no hesitation in rejecting, till the right word occurs which we recognise immediately. I think this is what Bion means by an 'empty thought'. It is also something which, though it cannot be imagined, can be described as analogous, say, to a form waiting for a content.

(Money-Kyrle, 1968, p. 692)

From the beginning of life, there is a "couple". Winnicott, for example, writes, "There is no such thing as an infant, meaning of course that whenever one finds an infant one finds maternal care" (Winnicott, 1958/1975, p. xxxvii).

Thus, along with the biological drive to seek out an "other", seen in other animals too, there is in the human infant the unconscious phantasy of there being an "other" with whom the infant links or seeks attachment (Fairbairn, 1946/1952; Bion, 1962, 1963; Money-Kyrle, 1968, 1971; Bowlby, 1969). From another perspective, developments in neuroscience have evidenced the neurobiological underpinning of attachment and romantic relationships. "Neuroscience illustrates the basic human need to connect to others, and how our thoughts, emotions, and behaviours – brain based activities reliant upon multiple neural pathways – underlie the nature of those connections" (Hiller, 2024).

Both psychoanalytic models of early development, that of holding and containment, illustrate how fundamental to existence this first couple is. Through being held in the relationship with the mother or primary carer, the infant can be supported by an environment within which maturation can occur. The infant is enabled to psychologically grow through the process of the mother/primary carer, who makes their mind and body available to contain the infant's primitive anxieties. This is a template for the idea that it is through linking with another that one can better understand oneself and the world, a development which later forms part of being a "creative couple" (Morgan, 2005).

As described earlier, psychic development takes a different trajectory for each person. Where there has been the provision of a good enough holding environment, sufficient containment and secure attachment, the individual will have a foundation to support new developments later in life, including that of becoming a couple. Some will have had more adverse experiences, for example, a primary caregiver who too often projects their own unmanageable experience into the infant, or a mentally unwell parent who does not have the capacity to provide the mind nor the facilitating environment that the infant needs. In such situations, the growing person is likely to struggle with being able to manage their own emotional states and to be able to think and reflect on their own feelings, and the feelings of others.

These early difficulties are likely to re-emerge later in various ways. The dependency needs that were not met in infancy may be sought in the new couple relationship, with an accompanying unconscious phantasy or belief that the other is responsible for meeting one's needs. This could result in a struggle between them of "who is to be the baby" (Lyons & Mattinson, 1993, p. 108), in a search for a containing or holding other.

Without having had the support to develop one's own separate sense of self, it might be difficult to conceive of the other as someone separate, with their own different mind and body. In this situation, the members of the couple might create a merger in which they can create a phantasy of oneness.

The experience of a lack of holding, containment and secure attachment may reverberate in the adult couple relationship. Couples' repetitive quarrelling can be seen as an attempt by partners to intrusively project into each other. Where there has been a more disturbed infant-parent bond, the partners in the couple can experience the other as intrusively projecting into them. Early experiences of being projected into by the primary caregiver may also lead to the establishment of wall-like defences to prevent intrusion. The partner may then experience the other as impenetrable and unable to take in any of the other's emotional communications (Fisher, 1993; Morgan, 2010). In this dynamic, as in the one of merger, the partners may each have difficulty in establishing boundaries around the self. The individuals in such relationships can then feel confused about which feelings belong to whom.

Lucy and Joe, in couple therapy for several years, illustrate how their early experience of being cared for by a mentally unwell mother affected and impaired their intimate adult couple relationship later in life. For them, being part of a couple was felt to be emotionally dangerous, and each erected defences to protect themself from the other experienced as intrusive.

Clinical example: Lucy and Joe

This couple's level of anxiety was illustrated in the following session. They began by discussing how hard it was to talk. They felt so vulnerable if they turned to each other for understanding that they had to "meet" and "check in" before they could begin. Joe felt Lucy did this by getting him to agree that they would talk at an appointed hour, and they would sit at the kitchen table without the radio on, which was on most of the time. Lucy felt Joe would then move around the kitchen making coffee or attending to something else, which made her feel as if she did not exist. She was left sitting by herself trying to listen to him but unable to hear him properly, and feeling she was some kind of "listening machine" or "listening bucket".

Lucy's expressions further illuminate the couple's difficulty taking something in. One was subject to the other's evacuation as if they were a bucket. This also reflected a dynamic between them and me. They wanted me to take their experience in, but they were not at all sure about the process of me giving it back to them, whether it could be more digested and understood, or whether it would be returned attached to my own projections or with malign intent. Both Joe and Lucy seem to have experienced a lack of ordinary maternal containment. Joe felt he could not penetrate his mother's mind and was fearful of what lay behind what he perceived as her "glazed eyes". Lucy often could not get the response she needed from her depressed mother, and when she did get a response, she was not sure what belonged to her and what belonged to her mother. Later in therapy, she described the disturbing experience of feeling her boundaries dissolving and no longer knowing what she thought or felt or who she was. With these difficulties in relating, having an emotional "intercourse" with another did not feel safe.

For much of the time, they felt in a battle for survival in trying to find space to articulate their experience before the other took over. In this state of mind, in which each felt desperation about being heard properly, it was difficult for them to hear, or be curious about, what was going on between them (based on previously published material, Morgan, 2017, pp. 94–95).

The Oedipal situation: Becoming three

The Oedipus complex is a well-known discovery of Freud's which refers to the early relationship between the infant and mother/primary carer and then with the parental couple. It is a rich concept but one that has required revisiting to take account of cultural difference and to reconsider the development of sexual identity and sexual partner choice. Klein considered the Oedipus complex to start much earlier than Freud had stated, and this earlier Oedipus complex, referred to as the "Oedipal situation", is an important point in the development towards becoming a couple, regardless of the child's parental configuration and the way in which the child's sexual identity and sexual object choice are formed.

The Oedipal situation captures that point in development when the child becomes aware of there being different relationships that exist other than the exclusive one he or she felt with the primary caregiver. The reality of another couple, the parental couple (that has been there all along), can come as quite a shock; the world is no longer as it was before. However, this realisation allows for a reconfiguration of the internal world, as a different kind of space can open up, with different possibilities. Ronald Britton has described this as "triangular space" (Britton, 1989).

Up until this point in development, the child is subjectively part of a couple with the mother/primary carer. With the awareness of the triangular situation, there is now also, from the position of being outside a couple, the idea of a couple as an entity. A couple one can observe and a couple one can be part of and observed by another or others.

This development can occur regardless of whether a parental couple exists in external reality because as the child develops the world outside him opens up, and there is an awareness of a primary object who relates to a world outside the infant, a world of other relationships, interests, work and so on. The child might become more aware of a symbolic couple inside his or her primary object. This, Dana Birksted-Breen argues, is part of the mother's containing capacity that

> already combines both the maternal function of being with and the paternal function of observing and linking. To contain her infant, a mother ... has to receive the projections empathically (the maternal function) and also take a perspective on this (the paternal function).
>
> (Birksted-Breen, 1996, p. 651)

The development of a "third position" is an important capacity when later in life becoming part of a couple. The capacity to be both subjectively part of a couple and also at the same time to observe oneself as part of that co-created relationship has been termed a "couple state of mind" (Morgan, 2001, 2019). A couple state of mind can help the partners move from a two-person dynamic in which each is focussed on the other in relation to the self, to one in which from a third position they can reflect on what they are creating together.

Whilst the Oedipal situation potentially brings about important psychic developments in the individual that facilitate forming a couple and being part of a couple, Oedipal dynamics never disappear and in fact can be particularly stimulated in a couple relationship. For example, the Oedipal feelings of exclusion, loss and jealousy whilst originating early in life are likely to be re-encountered later. The birth of the first child and the re-creation of "three", although usually a joyful experience, also gives rise to feelings of loss, exclusion and jealousy. The couple may feel they have lost their exclusive twosome; one partner may feel on the outside of the other parent and infant and feel jealous of the intimacy that is expressed between that pair. These feelings may reappear in later life too; for example, as Catriona Wrottesley points out, "The grandparental couple, like the child, must stand outside of the procreative young couple's relationship, and look upon what they cannot have" (Wrottesley, 2017, p. 193).

Affairs are not uncommon in a monogamous couple relationship, and feelings of betrayal and broken trust can take a
long time to recover from and sometimes cannot be. There are
also other forms of couple relationships that can give rise to
these feelings; open relationships, in which the sexual relations
with someone outside the primary couple, can develop unex-
pectedly into emotional intimacy. In polyamorous relationships,
the members are often not equal, some members of the polyamorous group having access to more partners than others, or
some being on the outside of a central couple. Jealousy and
feelings of exclusion, though not wanted or condoned, may be
hard to resolve.

Adolescence

Adolescence for most young people is a turbulent time. Powerful
sexual feelings and changes to the body can be experienced as
confusing and frightening. Working out what to do with a new
adult body can be very daunting for a young person. Stokoe
emphasises this point when drawing on the work of Moses
Laufer (1981); he writes, "the adolescent task is to take possession of the adult sexual body" (Stokoe, 2023, pp. 206–207).
Emotionally there is a need to reject and separate from parents
while also at times feeling very childlike and dependent on them.
There may be a lot of sexual exploration and experimentation or
alternatively fear and inhibition, and also figuring out one's
sexual identity – heterosexual, homosexual or bisexual being
only some of the possibilities.

The adolescent often has ambivalent feelings about the possibility of becoming part of a couple themself. It can be very hard to
relinquish being part of the group to be with one other. Witnes-
sing other members of the group making this development when
not ready to take this step oneself is also challenging. Hopefully
when this does occur, it is when there is a capacity to have enough
of a separate sense of self and a reasonably developed mind of
one's own, even though in the initial stages of being a couple there
may be a regressive merging component.

The creative couple

Psychic development doesn't cease on becoming part of a couple. It is not just about working through unresolved aspects of the past and not only about the psychic work required in dealing with the otherness of the other, which acts as an interference on each partner's subjectivity. A couple relationship itself can promote new creative developments. This is in part because the individual is faced with a paradox, that of being intimately connected with another who at the same time is "other" and to some extent unknowable. The creative couple capacity is one in which the members of the couple can tolerate the otherness of the other enough to be able to allow their different thoughts to interpenetrate. There is then the possibility of something previously unthought of and new to emerge.

The creative couple capacity is not a "once and for all" development, and it can be a hard psychic space to enter, since the otherness of the other may at times feel quite alien and therefore hard to engage with. The engagement itself also requires a capacity for negative capability (Keats, 1952), in which the outcome has not yet come into being and is not known. However, when possible, an outcome of this psychic "mating" can be one in which new thoughts and understanding are generated from the couple's unique link. The thirds that come into being, symbolised by the baby, could not have arisen in either of the members separately. Once this development is in place in a relationship, even though it is not available to the couple all the time, it can become a function of their relationship that they can re-find when needed. In this way, the relationship in the mind of each partner is experienced as a potential resource (Morgan, 2005).

References

Berenstein, I., Katz, B. & Filc, J. (2012). Vínculo as a Relationship between others. *Psychoanalytic Quarterly*, 81: 565–577.

Bion, W. R. (1962). *Learning from Experience*. London: Karnac.

Bion, W. R. (1963). *Elements of Psycho-Analysis*. London: Heinemann.

Birksted-Breen, D. (1996). Phallus, penis and mental space. *International Journal of Psycho-Analysis*, 77: 649–657.

Bowlby, J. (1969). *Attachment and Loss: Volume I: Attachment*. The International Psycho-Analytical Library, Vol. 79 (pp. 1–401). London: Hogarth Press and the Institute of Psycho-Analysis.

Britton, R. (1989). The missing link: Parental sexuality in the Oedipus Complex. In: J. Steiner (Ed.), *The Oedipus Complex Today: Clinical Implications* (pp. 83–101). London: Karnac.

Fairbairn, W. D. (1946/1952). Object-relationships and dynamic structure. In: *Psychoanalytic Studies of the Personality* (pp. 1–297). London: Tavistock Publications Limited.

Fisher, J. (1993). The impenetrable other: Ambivalence and the Oedipal conflict in work with couples. In: S. Ruszczynski (Ed.), *Psychotherapy with Couples: Theory and Practice at the Tavistock Institute of Marital Studies* (pp. 142–166). London: Karnac.

Hiller, J. (2024). *Sex in the Brain: A Neuropsychosexual Approach to Love and Intimacy*. Confer Books.

Keats, J. (1952). *Letters* (M. Forman, Ed.). London: Oxford University Press.

Laufer, M. (1981). The psychoanalyst and the adolescent's sexual development. *The Psychoanalytic Study of the Child*, 36: 181–191.

Lyons, A. & Mattinson, J. (1993). Individuation in marriage. In: S. Ruszczynski (Ed.), *Psychotherapy with Couples: Theory and Practice at the Tavistock Institute of Marital Studies* (pp. 104–125). London: Karnac.

Money-Kyrle, R. (1968). Cognitive development. *International Journal of Psycho-Analysis*, 49: 691–698.

Money-Kyrle, R. (1971). The aim of psychoanalysis. *International Journal of Psycho-Analysis*, 49: 691–698.

Morgan, M. (2005). On being able to be a couple: The importance of a "creative couple" in psychic life. In: F. Grier (Ed.), *Oedipus and the Couple* (pp. 9–30). London: Karnac.

Morgan, M. (2001). First contacts: The therapist's "couple state of mind" as a factor in the containment of couples seen for initial consultations. In: F. Grier (Ed.), *Brief Encounters with Couples* (pp. 17–32). London: Karnac.

Morgan, M. (2010). Unconscious beliefs about being a couple. *Fort Da*, 16 (1): 36–55.

Morgan, M. (2017). A couple case seen at Tavistock Relationships. In: D. E. Scharff & E. Palacios (Eds.). *Family and Couple Psychoanalysis: A Global Perspective* (Chapter 6). London: Karnac.

Morgan, M. (2019). *A Couple State of Mind: Psychoanalysis of Couples and the Tavistock Relationships Model*. London & New York: Routledge.

Ogden, T. (1994). *Subjects of Analysis*. Northvale, NJ: Jason Aronson.

Stokoe, P. (2023). Curiosity vs beliefs: The battle for reality and what this means for relationships and development. The 27th Enid Balint Memorial Lecture. *Couple and Family Psychoanalysis*, 13 (2): 196–211.

Winnicott, D. W. (1958/1975). *Through Paediatrics to Psychoanalysis: Collected Papers*. The Institute of Psychoanalysis. London: Karnac.

Winnicott, D. W. (1965). The theory of the parent-infant relationship (1960). *The Maturational Processes and the Facilitating Environment: Studies in the Theory of Emotional Development*, 64: 37–55.

Wrottesley, C. (2017). Does Oedipus never die? The grandparental couple grapple with "Oedipus". *Couple and Family Psychoanalysis*, 7 (2): 188–207.

Zinner, J. (1988). Projective identification is a key to resolving marital conflict. Unpublished paper.

Chapter 3

The interpersonal: Part I

Unconscious choice of partner, a
couple projective system,
interference and uncertainty

The central focus of all contemporary psychoanalytic approaches to couple relations is that which a couple co-create between them. For the couple analyst, this is represented by the expression that "the patient is the couple" – i.e., the relationship jointly created by the two partners. Within the Tavistock model, there are several concepts that explore this; for example, "unconscious choice of partner", "couple fit", the "couple projective system", the "couple transference relationship" and "shared unconscious phantasy". Shared unconscious phantasy and the development of this concept as "unconscious beliefs about a couple" will be explored in the next chapter.

The link perspective provides another lens on what is co-created, in that as well as the pull of transference and repetition, there is also the effect of "interference" and the idea of "uncertainty" as a regulator of the link between two people. The real "presence" of an other is seen as an "interference" acting on the preconceptions of the other subject.

Thus, what is co-created in a couple's unconscious relations can be thought about from different dynamically interacting perspectives. The couple come together and form a bond through identification and recognising aspects of the self in the other, through a wish to work something through from the past or to form an alliance to defend against what feels too threatening. At the same time, the "alterity", of the self and the other, meaning the state of otherness in self and other, might disrupt the unconscious agreements and break free of the repetition. A fuller elaboration of the concept of alterity in couple relations can be found in Chapter 2

DOI: 10.4324/9781003352518-4

of Pickering's book *Being in Love: Therapeutic Pathways through Psychological Obstacles to Love* (2008).

Projective identification, unconscious choice of partner and couple fit

The idea of unconscious choice of partner suggests that couples are unconsciously drawn together by factors which they may be unaware of. These may be thought of as the unconscious components to the conscious experiences of falling in love, sexual attraction and psychological connection. Couples sometimes describe finding their "other half" or their "soulmate". In fact, this might be a good description of some of the unconscious processes that are occurring. It is as if, through the intimate connection with another, there is a feeling of reconnecting with parts of the self, and this can be a powerful experience driving choice of partner.

The early clinicians within the Tavistock approach sought to understand this and utilised the psychoanalytic concept of projective identification. Melanie Klein saw projective identification as a defensive process, a primitive phantasy in which parts of the self that felt unmanageable were split off from the self and projected into another, initially by the infant into the mother or primary carer. The other was then seen as embodying these split off parts, now no longer felt to be part of the self but instead part of the other (Klein 1946, 1952).

The concept of projective identification has been developed significantly and very creatively since Klein's original conceptualisation. In contemporary analytic thinking, it is understood not as a solely intrapsychic process but as an interpersonal process, as a defence, as a mode of communication, as a way of relating and as the basis for empathy. In couples and other relationships, projective identification can also be part of creating a narcissistic relationship in phantasy whereby the otherness of the other is denied or minimised. This can lead to various forms of "narcissistic pacts" in the way a couple functions together, such as that seen in a "projective gridlock" (Morgan, 1995, see also Chapter 5).

This expansion of the concept has led some writers to distinguish between these very different forms of projective identification and name them accordingly. While Klein saw projective identification as a defensive process occurring intrapsychically, Bion saw that what the infant split off and projected could be a primitive form of communication – between the infant and the mother or primary carer.

Donald Meltzer considered it appropriate to differentiate between these rather different processes. For Klein, projective identification was about expelling unwanted parts of the self into the other, where it is hoped they will stay, and this is rather different to Bion's idea of projective identification, which although defensive in part is also a means of communicating undigested feelings in the hope that they might be later returned in manageable form. For Bion's development of the concept, Meltzer suggested retaining the term projective identification, and for Klein's original use of projective identification, he suggested the term "intrusive identification" (Meltzer, 1986, p. 69). Both kinds of projective processes can be observed in couple relations and can create very different kinds of projective systems.

Projective identification and the couple projective system as a form of communication

Projective identification is an unconscious process and cannot be perceived directly. It can, however, be experienced through the feeling states of the projector and the person projected into. For example, projected envy can leave the projector feeling and believing that "I don't have an envious bone in my body" and the projected into other feeling unsettled by uncomfortable envious feelings of which they were previously not feeling. In this intrusive form of projective identification, unwanted feelings in the self are evacuated into another in unconscious phantasy. Through subtle unconscious dynamics in the couple's relating, these are kept at bay by the subject and stimulated in the other.

By way of contrast, Ogden helpfully elucidates the communicative and developmental form of this process (distinguishing it from projective identification, which for him, unlike Meltzer, is retained for

Klein's original defensive process) in a way that can be thought about as the mechanism occurring in couple relations:

> The elicited feelings are the product of a different personality system with different strengths and weaknesses. This fact opens the door to the possibility that the projected feelings (more accurately, the congruent set of feelings elicited in the recipient) will be handled differently from the manner in which the projector has been able to handle them ... These methods of dealing with feelings contrast with projective identification in that they are not basically efforts to avoid, get rid of, deny, or forget feelings and ideas; rather, they represent different types of attempts to live with, or contain, an aspect of oneself without disavowal. If the recipient of the projection can deal with the feelings projected 'into' him in a way that differs from the projector's method, a new set of feelings is generated which can be viewed as a 'processed' version of the original projected feelings. The new set of feelings might involve the sense that the projected feelings, thoughts, and representations can be lived with, without damaging other aspects of the self or of one's valued external or internal objects (cf. Little, 1966).
>
> (Ogden, 1979, pp. 360–361)

In a couple relationship, each partner has, as Ogden points out, a personality system with different strengths and weaknesses. In a containing relationship, there may be a willingness in each partner to carry the other's projections temporarily or more or less permanently. Although unconscious, it might be as if one partner is saying to the other, "I can't manage this feeling, or part of myself – so can you have it for me?" In the formation of a couple projective system, the other's willingness to receive these split off aspects and their capacity to manage them differently is observed by the projecting other. This may enable that partner to take back these aspects of the self over time.

This developmental potential in a couple relationship was also expressed by Douglas Woodhouse as a split off aspect of the self, "lived with" in the other.

Developmental (and therefore therapeutic) potential lies in the fact that what is feared and rejected in the internal world, and is located in the person of the partner, is not lost but it is 'lived with'. It is therefore available experientially and may be assimilated.

(Woodhouse, 1990, p. 104)

Dicks had also observed this mutual developmental projective identification process in couples, which he described as,

Unconscious complementariness, a kind of division of function by which each partner supplied part of a set of qualities, the sum of which created a complete dyadic unit. This joint personality or integrate, enabled each half to rediscover lost aspects of their primary object relations, which they had split off or repressed, and which they were, in their involvement with the spouse, re-experiencing by projective identification.

(Dicks, 1967/1993, p. 69)

These arrangements came to be thought about as a couple's developmental "shared projective system", which could be thought of as part of an unconscious agreement between the couple. Embedded in this concept is the idea that individuals can work through and re-introject unresolved or conflictual aspects of themselves, and together the partners can create a relationship that enables this development. Couple relationships provide a special opportunity to re-integrate parts of the self, since the parts are projected into someone who is (usually) lived with on a daily basis.

Defensive forms of projective identification and couple projective systems

The process of mutual projective identification is not always one that leads to growth in each individual partner, in which parts of the self are processed in the other and re-introjected. The individual may have constructed his or her personality around certain unconscious beliefs; for example, the idea that "vulnerability is weakness", and choose a partner who expresses vulnerability on

his or her behalf. In that way, the vulnerable part of the self projected into the other is in close proximity to the self, though that
part is too feared to be taken back. In this kind of dynamic, one
can observe how an apparently strong partner ministers to the
vulnerable other, thereby keeping this unacknowledged part of the
self alive but at a manageable distance from the self. The relationship is unconsciously constructed and maintained in a way
that defends against these problematic internal conflicts that the
projector cannot come to terms with.

Sometimes the projected feeling, for example anger, meets with the
other partner's own anger, so that the recipient of the projection
carries what has been a called a "double dose" (Pincus, 1962, p. 18;
Cleavely, 1993, p. 65). The double dose of feelings may not feel
manageable to the partner who has been projected into. Instead of
that feeling being contained and eventually felt to be more manageable by the projector, and available for re-introjection, the couple can
become very split, with one partner prone to angry outbursts. This
reaction only makes the projecting partner more frightened of their
own (projected) anger and in fact more determined to keep this
unmanageable feeling in the other. Subtle manipulations of the
partner can be used to maintain the unwanted anger in the pro-
jected-into partner, whilst another set of feelings, perhaps depression,
could be split off and projected by the other.

Jürg Willi (1984) saw that couples could collude in this way to
avoid shared areas that make them anxious. He also observed the
potential for polarisation, through each member of the couple
carrying opposite aspects of a shared theme or issue.

> Partners may feel attracted by a mutually fascinating yet at the
> same time disturbing theme ... . Often unconsciously, these
> central themes constitute the common basis of marital relations.
> Similar fears may cause the build-up of a reciprocally organised
> defensive system helping both partners to neutralize these fears,
> to compensate for offenses, and to avoid or master threatening
> situations. The consequence may be a collusion, an unconscious,
> neurotic interplay of two partners that is based on similar,
> unresolved, central conflicts and acted out in polarized roles.
>
> (Willi, 1984, p. 179)

In other relationships, each partner projects similar unmanageable aspects into the other which neither can contain, and what results is escalating cycles of projection and re-projection.

Clinical example: Matt and Abe

This couple who came for help was very keen to understand what was going wrong in their relationship; they could not understand how easily communication broke down between them. In one session, Matt told the therapist, "There's another problem with how we communicate. Where I get caught is often when Abe seems anxious yet may be unaware of this. I have recently realised how anxious I then feel. I then get very anxious that I can't take his anxiety away." Abe responded, "We are both anxious people, but sometimes I think I'm handling something fine, you know, like when we lost your house keys, but then I find you are filling me with anxiety almost like you're enjoying it!" Matt immediately followed with, "But that's the thing Abe, you don't seem to realise how anxious you really are …". As the couple interacted, the therapist could feel the anxiety escalating in the room (Morgan, 2019, pp. 101–102).

Behind some couples' conflicts is this mutual attempt to project a similar unmanageable feeling into the other. In this situation, it is almost impossible to contain the other's projections, as each partner feels attacked by them. The conflict can escalate, as the more impermeable the other is, the more forceful and aggressive the projections become. Alexandra Novakovic understands this dynamic to be at play in couples who engage in "repetitive quarrelling". She noted that,

> although the couple is engaged in a verbal exchange, the language is used as a form of action, to act out and evacuate disturbing experiences. In arguments of this kind, partners do not want to know about their own or their partner's emotional experience, nor about the nature of the relationship between them.

(2016, p. 85)

Novakovic witnessed that the exchange between the couple can take on sadistic and excited qualities as psychotic anxieties are mutually projected to defend against the experience of pain, helplessness and depression. Quoting Bion, she suggests that couples get caught up together in a way of relating in which boundaries between the two become lost,

> the psycho-analysis of such a patient soon reveals a complex 'situation' rather than a complex 'patient'. There is a *field of emotional force* in which the *individuals seem to lose their boundaries as individuals* and become 'areas' around and though which emotions play at will.
>
> (Bion, 1967, p. 146, cited in Novakovic, 2016, p. 99; her emphasis added)

In thinking about projective identification in couple relations, it is easy to focus on the projector as the main actor, as each partner seeks to defensively keep a part of the self located in the other, or in a more developmental relationship, work it through in the safety and intimacy of the relationship and be able to eventually re-introject it. However, in some more disturbed relationships, it might also be that a projected aspect is neither contained nor re-projected by the other but "taken over" by them. For example, sometimes individuals with a poor sense of self are drawn to very narcissistically self-assured partners. It can look like there is a weak partner and a strong partner, the weaker one often ceding to the views of the strong one. As the weaker one develops, the one with the stronger personality is unwilling to give back the perceived to be positive capacities of the partner that have been projected into him or her, since the narcissistic personality is also in fact vulnerable and needs the projection of strength from the other. Britton described this form of projection as "acquisitive", to differentiate it from the more usual attributive form. "In acquisitive identification, the phantasy is *I am you*; in attributive identification, it is *You are me*" (Britton, 2003, p. 167, emphasis in original). Christopher Bollas describes a similar process in his concept of "extractive introjection", "a procedure in which one person invades another person's mind and appropriates certain elements of mental life" (1987, p. 163), or in a couple relationship, a partner recognises something in the other that they don't possess and takes it over.

The couple transference relationship

The personal history of each partner and the psychic developments they have made from infancy onwards are always brought to bear on the current couple relationship. The transference relationship between a couple has been termed by Miguel Alejo Spivacow as "intra-couple transference", where the "bi-directionality confirms and feeds back the transference projections" (Spivacow, 2019, p. 101). Couples sometimes talk about their "personal baggage" brought into a relationship, suggesting that there is some awareness of this for some. Pickering, in considering traumatic experiences in the lives of the partners, or those carried over from previous generations, describes how they are brought into the new relationship as a "malignant dowry" (Pickering, 2011).

Another way of thinking about unconscious choice of partner is about repetition and transference. A repetition of an early, unresolved relationship or internal versions of this was noted by Freud in *Beyond the Pleasure Principle*. He gives examples of individuals whose relationships all seem to have the same outcome, whereby a similar object is repeatedly chosen but nothing is worked through; no new relationship develops. For example, he speaks of, "the lover each of whose love affairs with a woman passes through the same phases and reaches the same conclusion" (1920, p. 22).

Lily Pincus, one of the pioneers of the Tavistock model, wrote in 1962:

> Although there is often a wish to start afresh in marriage and to escape the frustrations or disappointments of unsatisfactory early relationships, the strong unconscious ties to the first love-objects may help determine the choice of partner with whom the earlier situation can be compulsively re-enacted.
>
> (Pincus, 1962, p. 14)

Couples might consciously avoid the repetition of a previous problematic experience of relating; for example, by choosing someone who appears loyal and trustworthy unlike the father who had affairs and left the family, only to find they have unconsciously linked to a partner who repeats an earlier situation and betrays them in one way or another. The unconscious internal expectations of relating may contribute to creating that which is most feared.

Sometimes there is a conscious wish to create something different from the past or break free of constraints from the family of origin and the culture in which one grew up. However, it can sometimes happen that in choosing someone apparently very different – perhaps from another culture and/or ethnicity – one finds that a psychologically similar other has been chosen, and the relationship created is very familiar. As Neville Symington put it, "phantasy creates a response in the social environment and this is a constituent part of it" (Symington, 1985, p. 349).

In this sense, the new relationship becomes an actualised version of an earlier relationship.

Interference and uncertainty

The discussion of projective identification and transference in a couple relationship can take on a predetermined slant. For a projective system to develop, it is usually on the basis that the projections from one member of the couple are identified with and introjected by the other member, though other dynamics such as rapid re-projection or acquisitive identification may occur as described above.

However, although the aggregate that the couple creates is influenced by what each partner brings to the relationship, the way the partners in the couple then relate together and function takes on a life of its own. What happens between them can be difficult, disturbing and hard for them to process. The relationship the couple forms is not based solely on relating between subject and object, each seeing the other in ways determined by their respective inner worlds. Each partner's unconscious is shaped by different familial, cultural and social experiences and beliefs – the horizontal axis described in Chapter 1 – which comes together in the link the couple form. This aspect of their relationship – i.e., between subject and subject – is unlike the one based on identifications, repetition and working through. It is unknown and unpredictable.

What is newly created between the members of the couple is those elements of the other which cannot be assimilated into the various updated versions of the past, seen in transferential repetition. Some aspects of couple relations are determined by each subject's transference expectations and projections that are accepted by the other, but others are not. There might also be a resistance to fitting in with these unconscious pressures to be what each subject might need the other one to be. Käes states the subject of the relationship is not only an object of projection but also "the end of a process of psychic exchange and, therefore, is like the other subject, another subject who does insist and does resist in so much as he is the other" (Käes 1994, p. 190, cited in Scharff & Palacios, 2017, p. 29).

Thus, the link perspective brings a helpful counterpoint to the idea of transference and repetition. This perspective suggests that the otherness of the other resists fitting into projections from the self and forces each member of the couple or link to deal with aspects of the other that are unpredictable and new. "Interference" is a concept that is juxtaposed to "transference" and describes a different process, that in which the "presence" of a real other in a relationship may resist an attempt to re-create what is known and familiar. The concept of interference is described by Berenstein, who along with Puget developed Pichon-Riviere's ideas in relation to couples and families.

> Interference, which is what is produced in the space in-between as a result of there being two or more subjects whose presence generates something new and unknown. The unknown forces these subjects to do something with it, to inscribe it and to attempt to produce a becoming based on difference while dealing with the uncertainty about what they may be able to achieve.
> (Berenstein, 2012, p. 576)

Another aspect highlighted by this approach is that the link the couple form is full of uncertainty and unpredictability. Although the couple may create a bond through making connections based

on what is familiar and shared, there is always something fundamentally unknown about what will be created in their link, the "in
between", which has not come into being before. It is newly created through the couple's encounter with one another. The link
perspective explores how this creates uncertainty in the relationship, as it cannot be known what the meeting of two psyches will
create. Puget states that "Every link bears a haphazard, unexpected, *unforeseen* potential born from the manifold ways in which
difference is produced between two or more subjects" (2010, p. 9).

The link perspective and the object relations perspective are
often represented as very different logics. That might be true, but a
study of unconscious couple relations reveals that both these processes are occurring in a couple relationship. To make a bond,
identification is important – i.e., feeling there is something known
and familiar in the other including shared values. It may also be
that choosing someone very different from one's family of origin
may feel essential, but there is still an expectation on the other to
meet this expectation of being different. There is also the seeking
of missing parts of the self in the other and another who is similar
to past figures with which one can work something through. Some
of the projections and transference expectations will be accepted
by the other, others will not. At the same time, the couple cannot
predict what will be created between them in their unique link,
which means that alongside the sense of familiarity in a relationship there is always unpredictability.

References

Berenstein, I. (2012). Vínculo as a relationship between others.
Psychoanalytic Quarterly, 81 (3): 565–577.
Bollas, C. (1987). *The Shadow of the Object: Psychoanalysis of the
Unthought Known*. London: Free Association Books.
Britton, R. (2003). *Sex, Death and the Superego: Experiences in
Psychoanalysis*. London: Karnac.
Cleavely, E. (1993). Relationships: Interaction, defences, and transforma-
tion. In: S. Ruszczynski (Ed.), *Psychotherapy with Couples: Theory and
Practice at the Tavistock Institute of Marital Studies* (pp. 55–69).
London: Karnac.

Dicks, H. V. (1967/1993). *Marital Tensions: Clinical Studies towards a Psychological Theory of Interaction.* London: Karnac.

Freud, S. (1920). *Beyond the Pleasure Principle.* In: The Standard Edition of the Complete Psychological Works of Sigmund Freud, Volume 18 (1920–1922): Beyond the Pleasure Principle, Group Psychology and Other Works (pp. 1–64). London: Hogarth Press.

Klein, M. (1946). Notes on some schizoid mechanisms. *International Journal of Psycho-Analysis*, 27: 99–110.

Klein, M. (1952). Notes on some schizoid mechanisms. In: M. Klein, P. Heimann, S. Isaacs & J. Riviere (Eds.), *Developments in Psycho-Analysis* (pp. 292–320). London: Hogarth Press.

Meltzer, D. (1986). *Studies in Extended Metapsychology: Clinical Applications of Bion's Ideas.* London: Karnac.

Morgan, M. (1995). The projective gridlock: A form of projective identification in couple relationships. In: S. Ruszczynski & J. V. Fisher (Eds.), *Intrusiveness and Intimacy in the Couple* (pp. 33–48). London: Karnac.

Morgan, M. (2019). *A Couple State of Mind: Psychoanalysis of Couples and the Tavistock Relationships Model.* London & New York: Routledge.

Novakovic, A. (2016). The quarrelling couple. In: A. Novakovic (Ed.), *Couple Dynamics: Psychoanalytic Perspectives in Work with the Individual, the Couple and the Group* (pp. 85–105). London: Karnac.

Ogden, T. H. (1979). On projective identification. *International Journal of Psycho-Analysis*, 60: 357–373.

Pickering, J. (2008). *Being in Love: Therapeutic Pathways through Psychological Obstacles to Love.* London & New York: Routledge.

Pickering, J. (2011). Bion and the couple. *Couple and Family Psychoanalysis*, 1 (1): 49–68. London: Karnac.

Pincus, L. (1962). The nature of marital interaction. In: The Institute of Marital Studies (Ed.), *The Marital Relationship as a Focus for Casework* (pp. 13–25). London: Institute of Marital Studies.

Puget, J. (2010). The subjectivity of certainty and the subjectivity of uncertainty. *Psychoanalytic Dialogues*, 20 (1): 4–20.

Scharff, D. E. & Palacios, E. (Eds.) (2017). *Family and Couple Psychoanalysis: A Global Perspective.* London: Karnac.

Spivacow, M. A. (2019). Therapeutic intervention in psychoanalytical clinical work with couples. In: T. Keogh & E. Palacios (Eds.), *Interpretation in Couple and Family Psychoanalysis: Cross Cultural Perspectives* (pp. 92–102). London: Routledge.

Symington, N. (1985). Phantasy effects that which it represents. *International Journal of Psycho-Analysis*, 66: 349–357.

Willi, J. (1984). The concept of collusion: A combined systemic-psycho-dynamic approach to marital therapy. *Family Process*, 23 (2): 177–185.
Woodhouse, D. (1990). The Tavistock Institute of Marital Studies: Evolution of a marital agency. In: C. Clulow (Ed.), *Marriage: Disillusion and Hope* (pp. 69–119). London: Karnac.

Chapter 4

The interpersonal: Part 2

Shared unconscious phantasy and beliefs, unconscious alliances and curiosity

A psychoanalytic concept that has been central in the Tavistock approach has been that of "shared unconscious phantasy". One of the ways unconscious phantasy subsequently developed was through the concept of "unconscious beliefs" (Britton, 1998) and then how it applied to being a couple (Morgan, 2010). The concept of unconscious beliefs about being a couple might also resonate with some aspects of the link perspective. Connected to the concept of shared unconscious phantasy is that of "a shared defence" that the couple set up to counter anxieties that stem from their shared phantasies. The concept of "unconscious alliances" (Käes, 1994), while broader than the idea of shared defence, also has some resonances with it.

Unconscious phantasy

For Klein, unconscious phantasy is ever present throughout life, accompanying all conscious activity. From the beginning of life, the infant has phantasies of what is happening to him; for example, the experience of hunger or discomfort, the presence and absence of the mother or primary object and sometimes primitive anxieties such as feelings of disintegration. At the beginning, the infant only has rudimentary ways of making sense of his experience – his internal states and the impact of the external world. Gradually, the developing individual begins to form ideas about what the world is like and to test them out in relation to reality, which may or may not confirm the phantasies. For example,

DOI: 10.4324/9781003352518-5

though the young infant may have the unconscious phantasy of being abandoned when the breast doesn't appear at the right moment, the experience of the breast reappearing time and time again might change the unconscious phantasy to one in which abandonment is temporary and the breast is still there. Thus, the relationship between unconscious phantasy and reality is a crucial one for growth and development. In health, these unconscious phantasies are amenable to change, as new experiences bring the primitive anxieties into better contact with reality. However, subsequent experiences of reality in which there is an unreliable or abandoning other may confirm the primitive anxiety and – if frequent enough – lead to insecurities continuing through life. Such phantasies may become more fixed and less amenable to modification by new experiences, taking the form of "unconscious beliefs" (Britton, 1998).

In an adult couple relationship, unconscious phantasy affects how each partner perceives and experiences the other. It is almost as if there is another unconscious conversation occurring alongside conscious communication. The partners in a couple can sometimes experience an event in entirely different ways, with hardly any agreement about what occurred. Unconscious phantasy and the way in which it colours external reality throws light on the misperceptions and misunderstandings that exist in all relationships. Although in many ways this is an ordinary fact of life, it can lead to conflict. Some of the worst arguments couples have are when they get in a state of mind in which each feels they have the hold on the reality of the event they are describing and the other does not. In this situation, as Fisher states, "it is important to keep in mind that, when we talk about the capacity to acknowledge the truth of our experience, we are talking about the truth of our emotional experience, the meaning, the emotional meaning, of our experience" (Fisher, 1999, p. 53).

The effect of unconscious phantasy can be quite powerful in creating the expected response in the other. In other words, the way one experiences the external world and through unconscious phantasy the subsequent way one relates to it often generates in another person the expected response, thereby confirming one's phantasies. For example, a partner in a relationship who feels sexually rejected by the other may unconsciously behave in ways that cause the other to sexually reject them. This can happen even when each partner feels sexually attracted to the other and they both want to have sex. An example I have given previously of a heterosexual couple illustrates this:

> One partner delaying coming up to bed at the time the other does can be experienced by that other as sexual rejection, loss of love or anger. Sometimes these are transient unconscious phantasies having their roots in an earlier experience in the relationship and experiences before the relationship. They could take a grip but if the other partner arrives in the bedroom the phantasy might recede – reality has an influence, and another unconscious phantasy might present of a couple who do sometimes have sex and still feel sexually attracted to each other.
>
> (Morgan, 2019, pp. 56–57)

However, as Symington shows, the other can be induced to confirm one's unconscious phantasy (Symington, 1985). The partner's lateness is felt to confirm a lack of love or sexual desire. The waiting partner's unconscious phantasy holds sway so that the other's overture is missed. Unconscious phantasy feels real to the individual, who may seek confirmation in external reality. Thinking about this dynamic from a couple point of view requires considering both partners' unconscious phantasies and beliefs about what the couple are creating together. It might be that the partner delaying coming to bed may feel anxious about his potency and his anxious hesitancy may be interpreted as disinterest by the other. It might be that this couple have a shared unconscious phantasy that sex is dangerous – i.e., it evokes feelings of intrusion or engulfment – and that they have unconsciously set up a shared defence (the early or lateness to bed, the hesitancy of sexual approach), which, while frustrating them, protects them against these anxieties.

Shared unconscious phantasy and shared defence

As with other concepts in the Tavistock model, which started with psychoanalytic concepts about an individual, a developing understanding of two people in a relationship generated new couple concepts. An important conceptual shift was made from thinking about the unconscious phantasies of each partner, to the understanding that an unconscious system was created in which the members of the couple act on each other and shape a shared unconscious relationship. This shift is part of the development of the idea of a couple creating a shared inner world. Hewison, in an historical overview of the concept of shared unconscious phantasy, notes that it was Kathleen Bannister and Lily Pincus who grasped the idea of unconscious phantasy as properly "shared" (Pincus, 1962; Bannister & Pincus, 1965; Hewison, 2014).

> [T]he unconscious residues in the personality of earlier conflicts, phantasies which are charged with anxiety or guilt, may 'match up' so that each partner reacts to the other in ways which perpetuate rather than resolve the conflicts and intensify the phantasies which they dare not risk putting to the test of reality.
>
> (Pincus, 1962, pp. 14–15)

Christopher Vincent believed that "most formulations of shared phantasies are expressed in terms of primitive anxieties about the survival of the self" (Vincent, 1992). An understanding of these shared primitive anxieties can throw light on the way a couple live out their relationship. For example, if a couple have a shared phantasy that dependency risks abandonment, the couple may create a shared defence in which they cling together and cannot allow the other an ordinary separate existence. Their shared defence whilst containing this anxiety to some extent also restricts the relationship.

Shared phantasies may not always affect the relationship in this way; it may be that the couple together are able to modify their shared phantasies through their interaction with external reality, which may not present itself in a way that confirms their phantasy.

Bannister and Pincus note that, "Shared phantasies and illusions exist in all marriages – but in those with less anxiety and more flexibility, the collusive interaction between the partners will be modified by the changing demands of life experiences" (Bannister & Pincus, 1965, p. 62).

Although some shared unconscious phantasies may grip a relationship and result in defences that constrain, others may be tested out and worked through by the couple, leading to development. Warren Colman, discussing shared unconscious phantasy and individuation, says:

> [T]hey should not be regarded merely as an impediment to the relationship but, rather, as its basic substratum, even its driving force. The question, as with Jung's archetypes, is whether the marriage is in the grip of its phantasies, to the extent of being lived by them, or is able to act as a developmental vehicle for them.
>
> (Colman, 1993, p. 128)

Thus, as with a couple's projective system (described in Chapter 3), the couple's shared unconscious phantasies may restrict the couple but may also trigger development in the relationship.

Unconscious beliefs

For unconscious phantasies that are more entrenched and less amenable to modification through contact with reality, Britton proposed the term "unconscious beliefs" (Britton, 1998). Following Klein's idea that some unreconstructed infantile phantasies remain in the deep layers of the unconscious in their unchanged original form, Britton describes the way in which a defence system builds up around the phantasy and the phantasy becomes a belief and part of the personality. A challenge to the belief is then felt as threatening, as this is experienced as a challenge to the self.

In a similar vein, Anthony Storr distinguishes between a hypothesis and a delusion. A hypothesis is more akin to an unconscious phantasy, as it can be tested out against reality and modified. A delusion is more akin to an unconscious belief because it does not become modified in this way and is defensive in nature. In Storr's terms, a "belief" has a different meaning to that of Britton's; it is more like an unconscious phantasy one is gripped by, but it doesn't have the fixed nature of an unconscious belief as in Britton's terms. For the latter, Storr uses the term "delusion".

> A hypothesis is, by definition, provisional; a notion which can be modified at any time by the discovery of new facts which do not support it. A belief is more emotionally toned, and requires a change, not only of thought, but of heart, to alter it. A delusion cannot be modified – for the whole personality is attacked if the delusion is undermined – and, whatever facts may be adduced against it, it remains unshaken. It is the emotional strength with which a delusion is held that is its chief characteristic – not its falsity. Every one of us has false beliefs; but these do not amount to delusions because they can be modified if necessity demands it. But delusions may be the only things which render life tolerable. And, as such, are jealously defended against all the assaults of reason.
>
> (Storr, 1960, pp. 14–15)

Storr describes clearly the way in which delusions create a defensive structure around and within the personality. In Britton's terms unconscious beliefs are felt in the unconscious as facts. Britton in recounting his shock when as a child he discovered that Father Christmas was not a fact but a belief of his realised,

> I needed the discovery that it was possible not to believe to discover that I had a belief and did not know a fact. It is the shift from thinking one knows a fact to realising one has a belief which is linked to self-awareness.
>
> (Britton, 1998, p. 14)

It is this capacity that can be so crucial for a couple developing insight into their relationship – the shift from thinking one knows a fact to realising one has a belief. It helps make sense of the emotional intensity accompanying some of the things couples say, argue about and feel distressed about. The following example is from a previous publication.

Clinical example

> *A husband started a session by complaining that he had hit a very low spot during the week and his wife did not give him the comfort and reassurance he needed. He felt extremely angry and upset about this. It was absolutely clear to me that I was to join in with his sense of outrage and explore with his wife her difficulty in supporting him. It felt that not to do so would be experienced as me holding some appalling alternative view that couples don't have to give each other emotional support. One could sympathise with his disappointment and wonder why she was unable or unwilling to provide this. However, if one has the concept of unconscious beliefs, then what also becomes very interesting is the particular emotional quality in the room – the fact that he felt so certain about this and there was no room to think about it, along with the pressure I felt in my countertransference to accept this belief. In fact, as I did try and look at this with them, rather than confirm his view, it made him more furious and he appealed to me incredulously – 'Look, isn't this what is supposed to happen in relationships?' Certainly, he seemed to think so. This is what an unconscious belief feels like – in his mind, at that moment it was simply a fact that a couple relationship should be like this.*
>
> (Morgan, 2010, pp. 37–38)

In couple relations, the belief system is often about the meaning of being part of a couple. Spivacow gives some typical examples of couple beliefs: "we have to tell each other everything"; "there can't be arguments when there is true love"; or "if they love each other and their new baby, there shouldn't be any ambivalence between them or with the child in their new life situation" (Spivacow, 2019, pp. 99–100).

Another such belief common amongst couples is elaborated by Monica Vorchheimer in a paper in which she describes couples' beliefs that they should "understand and be understood by each other". This expectation is not questioned. No one asks, "can we be attuned all the time, is that possible, or even desirable?" When the inevitable lack of this kind of attunement is encountered, something is felt to be wrong with the relationship. Meaning is ascribed to the ordinary limits on understanding, and this can take on a paranoid dynamic in a couple relationship. Vorchheimer says, "People would not think of themselves as victims of misunderstandings but exchanging lies; they think that misunderstandings are the result of second and hidden intentionalities and they do not conceive of them as unavoidable" (Vorchheimer, 2015, p. 9). These shared beliefs may have a conscious component (as in the examples above), but they are not questioned, as they are being driven unconsciously and are unchanged by contact with reality and sometimes supported by cultural and transgenerational beliefs. They form a backdrop to a couple's relating. Helen Tarsh and Elaine Bollinghaus (1999) described how these deeper shared unconscious phantasies (referred to here as unconscious beliefs) are very present in a relationship, shaping the couple's interaction but also, at the same time, very difficult to see.

> the deeper and more entrenched the phantasy, the more it suffuses the surface of the couple's interaction; yet the more elusive it will be to grasp, precisely because it is deeply unconscious and heavily defended against. In the consulting room it will be all around like the air that we breathe, but like the air it cannot be seen.
>
> (Tarsh & Bollinghaus, 1999, p. 126)

These ideas capture the way in which shared unconscious phantasies, and particularly shared unconscious beliefs, once created affect the interaction between the members of the couple. From the link perspective, this is resonant of a characteristic of the couple's unconscious link, described evocatively by Anna Nicolò and Diana Norsa: "These links constitute a background web that characterises interaction, like a stage on which the actors play their parts" (Nicolò & Norsa, 2017, p. 29).

Proleptic imagination

Fisher, writing within the Tavistock tradition, formulated the idea of a proleptic imagination. "In the proleptic imagination, whatever it is that is pictured, there is no space between the image or the idea and the fact or the reality" (Fisher, 2009, p. 35). The idea of the proleptic imagination throws light on the experience of relating under the sway of an unconscious belief that seeks confirmation in external reality and may distort external reality to conform with it. Actual reality cannot be utilised to modify the belief.

In a similar vein, Puget points to the tendency to predict to protect ourselves from things that happen. She describes how it is much easier to seek repetition rather than leave the future open. There is comfort in that which is familiar, predictable and certain.

> Uncertainty confronts us with the fragility of the present, with the imperfection of memory, with the presence of irreducible otherness. For this reason, the ego will likely protect itself from emerging anxiety either by resorting to the past (the known), or by constructing unshakeable truths.
>
> (Puget, 2010, p. 13)

Discovering something new can throw the individual off balance and disturb their psychic equilibrium, as described in the clinical papers of Betty Joseph (Feldman & Bott Spillius, 1989). A member of a couple can find it frustrating and disturbing when the other insists on seeing them in ways that are more about the internal mindset of the perceiver and less about the other as a different subject. When a couple are in the grip of an unconscious belief, it closes down on any experience of the other, or of external reality, that might challenge that belief. The following is an example from a previous publication.

> *A wife is waiting to meet her husband at the theatre; he doesn't turn up on time, she feels anxious. Soon she feels perhaps a bit paranoid – can everyone see that she is on her own, exposed and abandoned? Her fantasies about her husband begin to flourish, some conscious, some unconscious: he is with his female colleague, he is abandoning her in a cruel and humiliating way. They meet three quarters of an hour later, he having been stuck on the tube without mobile phone contact. What happens next is crucial for the couple. Can she recognise that her distress is about the impact of her unconscious beliefs and that they are beliefs but not facts? Or does her emotional experience so colour her experience of reality that, although he*

did not abandon her, it felt as if he did – and therefore her emotional reality is that he did. Emotionally there is a sense of conviction and certainty from which she cannot escape. Even though she might have some awareness that she is being driven by an unconscious belief, this awareness is not strong enough to counter the emotional impact of that unconscious belief. The couple then have a terrible evening in which she relates to him as if he has abandoned her.

(Morgan, 2010, pp. 40–41)

This example illustrates a further point about an unconscious belief – that there is a closing down of curiosity which, if it was enabled, might begin to counter the unconscious belief. They are "shutting out of the new, so that increasingly one must limit internal and external experience" (Schaefer, 2010, p. 59).

Shelley Nathans describes the proleptic imagination in action in a couple therapy in which both partners relate to each other through certainty. They create familiar stories which feel impossible to prise open. As she puts it:

This is also what gives many couple interactions a scripted quality. They know where this story is heading and where it will end. … Once a couple is caught up in such a dynamic, it can feel like there is no getting out of it; they are trapped, and we are trapped in the consulting room with them.

(Nathans, 2009, p. 59)

Unconscious alliances

Käes' concept of unconscious alliances refers to the bond co-created by the couple that also shapes the members of the couple, as they become part of the set they have created. In his words,

Unconscious alliances are one of the main formations of psychic reality that organise and characterise the consistency of links formed between several subjects, for example, in couples and in families, in groups and in institutions (Bracchi, 2011, Sommantico, 2011). Each one of us needs the other to realise those of our unconscious desires that are unattainable without the other, and vice versa. The goal of these alliances is to keep repressed, rejected, denied or erased, that which between each subject of a link can put the link at risk.

(Käes, 2016, p. 187)

Unconscious alliances have difference functions, but in their defensive form they might share some characteristics with the idea of a couple shared defence, a way of dealing with anxieties that the couple share and a way of protecting the relationship. The way in which unconscious alliances then influence the members of the couple is also resonant with the formation of shared unconscious beliefs that function in the background of a couple's relationship, unseen but directing the relationship.

Curiosity and unconscious beliefs

Philip Stokoe in his writing on curiosity likens unconscious beliefs to a fundamentalist state of mind (Stokoe, 2021). He explores the anxiety caused by uncertainty and not knowing. In the absence of containment, originally from the primary carer and later extending to society as a whole, a fundamentalist state of mind can provide a solution, but one that closes down thinking.

Unconscious beliefs, because of this sense of being a fact, are reassuring in the face of anxiety. They provide certainty. We all carry a number of such beliefs, explanations that ought to have been changed in the light of new experience but were retained instead. This unconscious denial of any evidence that might force us to change such a belief requires the withdrawal of curiosity. To put it another way, if there is to be any hope of challenging an unconscious belief, it begins with evoking curiosity.

(Stokoe, 2021, p. 197)

In couple relations, we see unconscious phantasy in the individual partners operating all the time, but this is amenable to change as the experience of the other and the world ceases to confirm them. In this way, there is a constant interplay between internal and external reality, and in health more alignment between the two. When unconscious phantasies are shared in a couple relationship, they may find confirmation in the defensive systems the couple create, but as Bannister and Pincus pointed out, the collusive interaction between the partners can be modified by the changing demands of external reality (Bannister & Pincus, 1965). Unconscious beliefs – or delusions, as Storr suggested – can become part of the personality. In couple relations, unconscious beliefs and delusions are often about the meaning of being part of a couple dealing with primitive anxieties, which Vincent alluded to on the topic of the survival of the self (Vincent, 1992). For these reasons, they are much harder to see and for the couple to break free of.

References

Bannister, K. & Pincus, L. (1965). *Shared Phantasy in Marital Problems: Therapy in a Four-Person Relationship*. London: Institute of Marital Studies.

Britton, R. (1998). *Belief and Imagination: Explorations in Psychoanalysis*. London: Routledge.

Colman, W. (1993). The individual and the couple. In: S. Ruszczynski (Ed.), *Psychotherapy with Couples: Theory and Practice at the Tavistock Institute of Marital Studies* (pp. 126–141). London: Karnac.

Feldman, M. & Bott Spillius, E. (Eds.) (1989). *Psychic Equilibrium & Psychic Change: Selected Papers of Betty Joseph* (pp. 181–193). London & New York: Tavistock/Routledge.

Fisher, J. (1999). *The Uninvited Guest: Emerging from Narcissism towards Marriage*. London: Karnac.

Fisher, J. V. (2009). Macbeth in the consulting room: Proleptic imagination and the couple. *Fort Da, 15* (2): 33–55.

Hewison, D. (2014). Shared unconscious phantasy in couples. In: D. E. Scharff & J. Savege Scharff (Eds.), *Psychoanalytic Couple Therapy: Foundations of Theory and Practice* (pp. 25–34). London: Karnac.

Käes, R. (1994). Psychic work and unconscious alliances in therapeutic institutions. *British Journal of Psychotherapy*, 10 (3): 361–371.

Käes, R. (2016). Links and transference within three interfering psychic spaces. *Couple and Family Psychoanalysis*, 6 (2): 181–193.

Morgan, M. (2010). Unconscious beliefs about being a couple. *Fort Da*, 16 (1): 36–55.

Morgan, M. (2019). *A Couple State of Mind: Psychoanalysis of Couples and the Tavistock Relationships Model*. London & New York: Routledge.

Nathans, S. (2009). Discussion of "Macbeth in the consulting room: Proleptic imagination and the couple", *Fort Da*, 15 (2): 56–65.

Nicolò, A. M. & Norsa, D. (2017). Brief introductions to theoretical and clinical approaches around the world. In: D. E. Scharff & E. Palacios (Eds.), *Family and Couple Psychoanalysis: A Global Perspective* (pp. 27–33). London: Karnac.

Pincus, L. (1962). The nature of marital interaction. In: The Institute of Marital Studies (Ed.), *The Marital Relationship as a Focus for Casework* (pp. 13–25). London: Institute of Marital Studies.

Puget, J. (2010). The subjectivity of certainty and the subjectivity of uncertainty. *Psychoanalytic Dialogues*, 20 (1): 4–20.

Schaefer, M. (2010). Discussion of "Unconscious beliefs about being a couple": Beliefs about a couple and beliefs about the other. *Fort Da*, 16 (1): 56–63.

Spivacow, M. A. (2019). Therapeutic intervention in psychoanalytical clinical work with couples. In: T. Keogh & E. Palacios (Eds.), *Interpretation in Couple and Family Psychoanalysis: Cross Cultural Perspectives* (pp. 92–102). London: Routledge.

Stokoe, P. (2021). *The Curiosity Drive: Our Need for Inquisitive Thinking*. London: Phoenix Publishing House.

Storr, A. (1960). *The Integrity of the Personality*. London: Heinemann.

Symington, N. (1985). Phantasy effects that which it represents. *International Journal of Psycho-Analysis*, 66: 349–357.

Tarsh, H. & Bollinghaus, E. (1999). Shared unconscious phantasy: Reality or illusion? *Sexual and Marital Therapy*, 14 (2): 123–136.

Vincent, C. (1992). Personal communication.

Vorchheimer, M. (2015). *Understanding the loss of understanding*. Paper presented at the IPA Congress, Boston.

Chapter 5

The interpersonal: Part 3

Narcissism and alterity

For intimacy to be truly alive, it requires a capacity for both togetherness and separateness. There is always, inevitably in any relationship, some tension between these different needs, and many couples struggle with this to some extent. Being close and together may be sought as a merger or may be feared as engulfment or claustrophobia. Being separate means facing the other's difference from oneself and their otherness, which cannot be subsumed into the self.

Difficulties in facing difference and otherness has caught the attention of couple psychoanalytic thinkers, as this aspect of relating is very common. The couple may feel that in being a couple they should be "on the same page", be in agreement, and be completely attuned in understanding and being understood by the other. This is not possible, but for some it can be hard to accept. It can result in excessive conflict as each partner seeks to encompass the other into their own way of being and seeing things. Or the couple may form various kinds of defensive arrangements to deal with the problem of otherness. It is a challenge that is inherent in couple relations.

Dynamics of separateness and togetherness

Narcissism ↔ Marriage

The Tavistock approach conceptualised the problem of separateness and togetherness as a dynamic between narcissistic and relational states. Fisher described this oscillation as that between narcissism and the psychological state of "marriage". By "marriage" he meant

DOI: 10.4324/9781003352518-6

a "state of object relating that can tolerate the tensions of the oscillation between oneness and separation" (1999, p. 220). In some relationships, we see a more entrenched or destructive narcissism in one or both partners. Fisher describes this as

> a kind of object relating in which there is an intolerance for the reality, the independent existence of the other. Narcissism in this sense is in fact a longing for an other, but a longing for an other who is perfectly attuned and responsive, and thus not a genuine other at all.
>
> (Fisher, 1999, pp. 1–2)

Here the emphasis is on the complex dynamic tension between making room for an other who really is "other", but at the same time holding on to one's own separate sense of self. Fisher believes this to be a challenging psychological task.

> The capacity to pursue the truth of one's own experience and also to tolerate the truth of another's experience, acknowledging and taking the meaning of the other's experience without losing the meaning of one's own, especially when these experiences not only differ but conflict, is a major developmental achievement.
>
> (Fisher, 1999, p. 56)

Relating and non-relating

Colman also saw a dynamic tension between togetherness and separateness, which he formulated as the movement between a capacity for relating and a need for non-relating. Colman conceptualised that there is an "anti-relating drive" alongside our "object seeking drive". However, he distinguishes "anti-relating" from "non-relating" – the latter is just as important as "relating" is in a relationship; in fact, it would be impossible to be actively relating to another all the time. Although one might argue that when we are in solitude we may be alone in the presence of another. "Being able to enjoy being 'alone' along with another person who is also 'alone' is in itself an experience of health" (Winnicott, 1958, p. 417).

For Colman,

[N]on-relating refers simply to the need for 'space' and solitude and is an inherent – and essential – aspect of all relationships. Relating to others is only tolerable within certain limits – beyond these we speak of 'intrusion' and 'invasion', an abrogation of our autonomy. We need not only to be close to others, but also to be separate from them, not only dependent but also independent. These needs amount to a need for non-relating, which in any successful relationship needs to be held in balance with the need for relating.

(Colman, 2005/2014, p. 23)

In couple relations, there is always a tension between one's own self-preoccupation and one's wish to relate to an "other" who is a separate and different person. Some writers have contrasted what can be described as a healthy narcissism with destructive narcissism. Ruszczynski argues that there is a healthy narcissism that exists alongside intimacy and that a good enough relationship needs to incorporate both (Ruszczynski, 2023). Thus, relating to another is not simply whether we open ourselves to another's experience or whether we maintain our own view, it is whether we can do both at the same time.

Similarly, Hanna Segal believes that self-love and love of the other are not mutually exclusive:

"The life instinct includes love of the self, but that love is not in opposition to a loving relationship to an object. Loving life means loving oneself and the life-giving object" (Segal, 1983, p. 275).

The developmental perspective in the Tavistock model also explores the process of individuation in couple relationships, in which over time, within a containing relationship, the members of a couple may gradually withdraw projections and become more psychically separate and whole. However, the process is never complete, since mutual projections also bind the couple.

The alienness of the other, presence, interference and imposition

Two of the writers from the link perspective who have addressed the otherness of the other in a compelling way are Berenstein and Puget. In their thinking about the alienness of the other (part of their elaboration of the link perspective in relation to couples), they emphasise the fact that part of the other remains alien and unknowable. Although identification with the other creates a bond, Berenstein saw that,

> Even in the similar and the different there is a part of the other that cannot be inscribed as the subject's own and which remains unknown – namely the alien, which is inherent in the presence of the other. ... In a significant relationship, it comprises every register of the other that the subject cannot succeed in inscribing as his own – yet, in the belief that this is possible, he must attempt to do so, until he finally accepts (albeit never completely) that it is an inherent characteristic of alienness that cannot be incorporated within the subject. This is the intrinsic, constitutive paradox of the link.
>
> (2001, p. 145)

It is important to note that the difficulty in accepting the alienness of the other is not seen as a narcissistic problem in itself but as a fact and something any couple must deal with – it is the work of the link. It is only when it cannot be dealt with that narcissistic solutions are sought.

Pickering cautions against an overemphasis on radical alterity, which she thought "can lead to a dualistic attitude, which brings in its wake a sense of alienation and separation in which no relation is possible" (2008, p. 41).

She also sees identification as existing in a dynamic relationship with alterity, stating, "Empathy aims to transcend and overcome the alienation created by difference and otherness: alterity has as its aim the recognition of and respect for diversity, the not-same and difference" (2008, p. 41).

The more we can come to terms with the otherness of the other, the greater is the stimulus which evokes a benign enquiry, our curiosity (Stokoe, 2021), and this leads to a deepening of the connection between the couple.

A central concept in the link perspective is the idea of the "presence" of the other and how the presence of the other impacts on the self. This concept was elaborated fully by Puget and Berenstein. Simply put, Berenstein defines it as follows: "Presence is the quality of the other that impacts powerfully on me as a subject or, if it is my presence, impacts on the other, impresses a stamp, and modifies both me and the other" (Berenstein, 2001).

If the "presence" of the other is too hard to manage, too disturbing to the subjectivity of the self, a process of "imposition" might occur, another concept from the link perspective. Unlike projective identification, in which a split off aspect of the self is attributed to the other, imposition is a different process. According to Berenstein,

> Imposition is a defensive action when the inhabitants of the link cannot tolerate the modification of their subjectivity by the fact of belonging to this relationship, and therefore resort to excessive imposition in order to abolish the alienness and turn it back into similarity.
>
> (Berenstein, 2001, p. 147)

Presence and interference are concepts related to the idea that however well a couple are relating, managing differences and even using their differences to be creative, there are always aspects of the other than cannot easily be integrated into the subject. Some aspects will always remain alien and unknowable. For the link perspective, this is a fundamental dynamic in couple relations and is part of the inevitable "suffering in the link" (Palacios & Monserrat, 2017, p. 63).

The seeking of attunement

Attunement between the members of a couple is an imperfect process, whether it is a mother/baby couple, or two partners in an intimate adult relationship. Winnicott aptly described the mother as "good enough" and the mother's capacity to gradually disillusion the infant as essential to development (Winnicott, 1971, p. 10). "Good enough" in Winnicott's terms does not imply a failure in the mother/primary carer but is seen as an important function enabling the infant to gradually adapt to the reality of non-perfect attunement. Yet for some couples the desire for perfect attunement may never get relinquished.

Any two people may find it hard to fully understand and feel sufficiently understood by the other. In adult couple relations, many needs, including those of a primitive nature, are expressed, and the emotional temperature can rise if one partner expresses their needs in ways that may feel overwhelming to the other. The other can become defensive and make the recipient feel that if they meet the needs of the other there will be no space for the needs of the self. Thus, there can be many failures to take in the other and feel taken in by the other. Even if the relationship is not emotionally volatile, there are ordinary difficulties in understanding an other.

In a healthy relationship, there is curiosity about the other and a wish to know them better. There is a relationship in which each partner feels they are with an other who wishes to understand them and sometimes achieves this. The capacity in the individual partners to bear being misunderstood and the capacity to be able to accept the limitations of one's own understanding of the other are further signs of a healthy relationship. For some, the failure to understand may be felt as a crisis in the relationship, a problem and an indication that there is something going wrong. In Vorchheimer's view, the idea that each partner can have a full understanding of the other is illusory and "is the effect of the narcissistic foundation of every couple" (Vorchheimer, 2015, p. 12).

This more disturbed experience of misunderstanding has been linked by Britton to the failure of maternal containment in early infancy, in which "one's experience of oneself would be eliminated". Instead of misunderstanding being experienced as disappointment or a deficiency in the other, it is felt as an attack, "a force is believed to exist that destroys understanding and eliminates meaning" (Britton, 2003, p. 176).

Britton also makes a useful link between the need for agreement in relation to the experience of being understood. "When there is a desire for understanding coupled with a dread of misunderstanding there is an insistent, desperate need for agreement in the analysis and annihilation of disagreement" (Britton, 1998, p. 57).

And later,

[T]he need for agreement is inversely proportional to the expectation of understanding. When expectation of understanding is high, difference of opinion is tolerable; where expectation of understanding is fairly high, difference of option is fairly tolerable; where there is no expectation of understanding the need for agreement is absolute.

(Britton, 1998, p. 57)

In couple relations, there are sometimes very emotionally dysregulated exchanges in which one partner is desperate for the agreement of the other. This sometimes manifests, for example, in views about how to bring up their children. If the other partner has a different view, it can feel unbearable to one who seeks agreement. That partner feels not only misunderstood but full of uncontained anxiety. This is a very different picture to a couple that feel secure enough to be able to bring their differences together in an attempt to find understanding and possibly a new way forward together. This is what is described in Morgan's concept of the "creative couple" (Morgan, 2005).

Narcissistic pacts

While all couples struggle to some extent with difference and otherness, for some this is a serious problem that has to be dealt with in some way. Different kinds of unconscious arrangements may be made between the members of the couple to manage this. Here I will outline some of the dynamic forms this can take, thought of broadly as different kinds of narcissistic pacts.

Oneness

Freud did not write very much about couple relations, though he did show considerable insight into some of them, including the experience of "oneness" when falling in love.

At the height of being in love the boundary between ego and object threatens to melt away. Against all the evidence of his senses, a man who is in love declares that 'I' and 'You' are one and is prepared to behave as if it were a fact.

(Freud, 1930, p. 66)

The experience of oneness is often heightened at this point. Couples do not usually come together and form a bond through facing the alienness of the other. The intimacy of the adult couple relationship can be felt as a reconnection to important early figures in one's life, particularly the early attuned intimate relation to the mother or primary carer that one had or longed for. Christopher Clulow and Maureen Boerma describe how in the early stages of a relationship the lovers engage in behaviour that is very reminiscent of the mother and baby bond:

> The state of being 'in love' is a kind of intoxication, desire a variant of addiction, and in this heightened state interpersonal boundaries buckle under the pressure from lovers to melt into and merge with each other. Falling in love, if not the psychosis that Freud would have it to be, certainly approximates a borderline condition.
>
> (Clulow & Boerma, 2009, pp. 81–82)

For most couples, this "psychotic" or "borderline" condition gradually gives way to something more reality based in which there is room for recognising and accepting differences, along with manageable love and hate. Despite the disillusionment that comes with seeing the other more realistically, there may still exist areas of "illusion" in the relationship that feel creative. Julie Friend describes this as a creative illusion:

> The beloved is, in some measure, both a part of oneself and a separate other, occupying in Alvarez' words, 'an intermediate area of experience in between pure narcissistic illusion that everything belongs to oneself and the mature awareness of separateness and indebtedness, where true symbolic functioning is possible' (Alvarez, 1996, p. 377).
>
> (Friend, 2013, p. 5)

However, for some couples the illusory state of oneness is maintained, often underpinned by an unconscious belief (see Chapter 4) in which they feel they are, and should be, more or less in total agreement. The couple seems to be drawn to creating a sense of oneness, functioning mainly through projective identification, as a way of continually maintaining the state of "I and you are one". Some couples exist this way for a while, and it may feel pleasurable, as unconsciously relating in this way serves the primitive needs of both.

This might be particularly exacerbated for those couples who collapse into more primitive psychic states, described by Ogden as the autistic-contiguous position (Ogden, 1994). Timothy Keogh and Sylvia Enfield, developing this concept in relation to couples, believed that between members of such couples "the sense of a bounded self with a psychic skin was not developed" (Keogh & Enfield, 2013, p. 44), and hence the collapse into the other.

One way in which this has been formulated is as a "projective gridlock" (Morgan, 1995). Here projective identification is used to create a sense for the couple of living inside each other, each partner feeling they know the other or are known by the other from the inside. The ordinary tension and conflict that are unavoidable in a relationship is, in phantasy, removed. However, this kind of relationship usually eventually becomes claustrophobic, at least for one of the partners, who starts to feel taken over by the other and loses a sense of who they are. As that partner withdraws from the gridlock, this can create an agoraphobic panic in the other, who feels they have nothing known to hold on to, as a significant part of the self that was lodged in the other is unlodged.

A sado-masochistic pact

Another type of narcissistic pact is more sado-masochistic in nature. One partner presents with a more obviously narcissistic, sometimes self-aggrandising self and the other with an undeveloped sense of self. The partner with the poor sense of self is attracted to the narcissistic certainty of the other and finds security in allowing themself to cling to the mind of the other. As with the projective gridlock, the narcissistic partner sometimes has the phantasy of knowing the other from the inside, sometimes believing they know the other better than the other knows themself. There is often an intrusive force in one partner and a lack of a boundaried self in the other, creating a dynamic in which one partner psychically takes over the other. Any hint of separateness can lead to sadistic controlling behaviour in one and masochistic submission in the other. Fisher describes the disturbing dynamics in this situation,

> The adhesive dynamics exacerbate masochistic tendencies, and the intrusive dynamics exacerbate sadistic tendencies, mutually reinforcing each other in the couple relationship as each partner feels increasingly locked into intensifying spirals of retaliation. The couple's folie à deux offers no way out.
>
> (Fisher, 1999, p. 243)

Clinical example: Mario and Lula

Mario and Lula came for a consultation as they felt their relationship, which had started off promisingly, was starting to unravel and both were very distressed. One issue they brought to the session was a disagreement about a holiday plan to stay with Mario's parents. Mario was keen on the plan, but Lula said she wanted time for the two of them without the intrusion of Mario's parents. As the session proceeded, Mario insisted more and more forcefully that this was not really what Lula wanted; they had agreed to join his parents, and this is what they often did and both wanted.

Lula started capitulating, and I remember noticing the position she started with began to unravel. Observing her, it felt like she was losing her own mind – her own thoughts were becoming lost as Mario's thoughts seemed to become inserted into her mind. I suggested to the couple that it might be very difficult for them to hold on to the different views they expressed at the beginning of the session. Mario angrily spoke over me, telling me, exasperated, that Lula really didn't know what she thought and relied on him.

I remember feeling this was such an extraordinary statement, but it was clear this was exactly as he thought, and Lula now seemed to have got herself into a psychic position in which she was in agreement with him. Now I was the only one with a different view.

It was a very powerful and disturbing experience to witness. I was also aware that I could not be allowed to have a separate mind, and my attempt to so – with the brief interpretation I made – could not be heard and probably fuelled a lot of anxiety in the couple (Based on a clinical example in Morgan, 2019, p. 94).

In this example, there is intrusive projective identification in the couple's relating. It is not about communicating an unprocessed feeling but about dealing with the anxiety that separateness and difference brings and controlling and taking possession of the other. Mario could not bear Lula's separateness, and this was clearly a very difficult position for her to occupy too. When Lula did something that highlighted that she did have a separate mind, Mario became very anxious and controlling. As is often the case in this kind of couple relationship, Lula had a very undeveloped sense of self and poor boundaries. She was attracted to Mario's seeming certainty, which she easily gave way to, as could be observed in the session.

A problem in sharing psychic space

Yet another kind of narcissistic pact is one in which the couple unconsciously agree that one of the partners will occupy the entire psychic space of the relationship and the other will remain outside it. Britton distinguishes between two kinds of narcissism: narcissistic detachment in which it is not possible to find a place within the psychic reality of the other and narcissistic adherence in which it is not possible to find a place outside it (Britton, 2003, p. 171). This dynamic can be observed in some couple relationships. The adherent and detached narcissist come together and create a particularly difficult dynamic, as the adherent narcissist cannot bear the separateness of the detached, and the detached narcissist is terrified of being drawn into the psychic reality of the adherent.

In these relationships, there is anxiety about bringing together difference linked to a fear of annihilation if there was a psychic intercourse between two minds (Britton, 2003). One way that this might be dealt with in a couple relationship is to make an unconscious agreement that one person's psychic reality colonises the marriage and the other's is kept entirely out of it, either split off from consciousness or secretly maintained.

What these last two narcissistic pacts have in common is that one partner often has a poorly developed sense of self, so it is very difficult for them to occupy a separate position in relation to the other. They are either very susceptible to the other's defining of them, as in the sado-masochistic pact, or they have a very limited capacity to define themself, encouraging a psychic takeover from the other. When one person is so afraid of knowing their own mind, it can allow the other to foster the illusion of sameness and agreement.

Curiosity and narcissism

Curiosity has been juxtaposed with narcissism just as it has with unconscious beliefs. Unconscious beliefs and narcissism share a state of mind in which not knowing causes anxiety and causes curiosity to be shut down (Morgan & Stokoe, 2014).

Several writers have contrasted curiosity with narcissism. Colman, for example, states,

> Curiosity is the opposite of narcissism. Where curiosity seeks to know, intrusiveness seeks to possess, to incorporate the unknown of the other into the boundaries of the self and so to abrogate the painful rubbing up against the reality of difference. Alternatively, the narcissistic person may claim to already know the other since what he actually sees and takes for the other is merely the reflection of his own projective identifications.
>
> (Colman, 2005/2014, p. 28)

This idea is also central in Fisher's work; he saw non-intrusive curiosity as fundamental to a deep and enduring love in the intimate couple relationship. Keeping curiosity alive can be challenging in long-term relationships. Familiarity in long-term relationships can provide security but might also make it difficult to keep curiosity alive. There is no room for surprise and yet sometimes there can be surprises that erupt and can threaten the relationship, a common example being an affair. If the affair can be recovered from, there might then need to be a process of re-discovering the other, oneself and each partner's assumptions about the relationship. Curiosity may need to be re-found or found.

References

Berenstein, I. (2001). The link and the other. *International Journal of Psycho-Analysis*, 82: 141–149.

Britton, R. (1998). *Belief and Imagination: Explorations in Psychoanalysis*. London: Routledge.

Britton, R. (2003). Narcissistic problems in sharing space. In: R. Britton, *Sex, Death, and the Superego: Experiences in Psychoanalysis* (pp. 165–178). London: Karnac.

Clulow, C. & Boerma, M. (2009). Dynamics and disorders of sexual desire. In: C. Clulow (Ed.), *Sex, Attachment and Couple Psychotherapy: Psychoanalytic Perspectives* (pp. 75–101). London: Karnac.

Colman, W. (2005/2014). The intolerable other: The difficulty in becoming a couple. *Couple and Family Psychoanalysis*, 4 (1): 22–41.

Fisher, J. (1999). *The Uninvited Guest: Emerging from Narcissism towards Marriage*. London: Karnac.

Freud, S. (1930). *Civilization and its Discontents*. In: The Standard Edition of the Complete Psychological Works of Sigmund Freud, Volume 21 (1927–1931): The Future of an Illusion, Civilization and its Discontents, and Other Works (pp. 57–146). London: Hogarth Press.

Friend, J. (2013). Love as a creative illusion and its place in psychoanalytic couple psychotherapy. *Couple and Family Psychoanalysis*, 3 (1): 3–14.

Keogh, T. & Enfield, S. (2013). From regression to recovery: Tracking developmental anxieties in couple therapy. *Couple and Family Psychoanalysis*, 3 (1): 28–46.

Morgan, M. (1995). The projective gridlock: A form of projective identification in couple relationships. In: S. Ruszczynski & J. V. Fisher (Eds.), *Intrusiveness and Intimacy in the Couple* (pp. 33–48). London: Karnac.

Morgan, M. (2005). On being able to be a couple: The importance of a "creative couple" in psychic life. In: F. Grier (Ed.), *Oedipus and the Couple* (pp. 9–30). London: Karnac.

Morgan, M. & Stokoe, P. (2014). Curiosity. *Couple and Family Psychoanalysis*, 4 (1): 42–55.

Morgan, M. (2019). *A Couple State of Mind: Psychoanalysis of Couples and the Tavistock Relationships Model*. London & New York: Routledge.

Ogden, T. H. (1994). The analytic third: Working with the intersubjective clinical facts. *International Journal of Psycho-Analysis*, 75: 3–19.

Palacios, E. & Monserrat, A. (2017). Contributions to the link perspective in interventions with families: Theoretical and technical aspects, and clinical application. In: D. E. Scharff & E. Palacios (Eds.), *Family and Couple Psychoanalysis: A Global Perspective*. London: Karnac.

Pickering, J. (2008). *Being in Love: Therapeutic Pathways through Psychological Obstacles to Love.* London & New York: Routledge.

Ruszczynski, S. (2023.) *So near and yet so far: Further thoughts on narcissism and the couple.* Lectures from the Tavistock Relationships Model. Unpublished.

Segal, H. (1983). Some clinical implications of Melanie Klein's work: Emergence from narcissism. *International Journal of Psycho-Analysis, 64*: 269–276.

Stokoe, P. (2021). *The Curiosity Drive: Our Need for Inquisitive Thinking.* London: Phoenix Publishing House.

Vorchheimer, M. (2015). *Understanding the loss of understanding.* Paper presented at the IPA Congress, Boston.

Winnicott, D. W. (1958). The capacity to be alone. *International Journal of Psycho-Analysis*, 39: 416–420.

Winnicott, D. W. (1971). *Playing and Reality.* London & New York: Routledge.

Chapter 6

The couple relationship as a third

The idea of the relationship as a "third", a co-created entity between the members of the couple, has been formulated in several ways from different psychoanalytic perspectives. There are different kinds of thirds in couple relations describing different kinds of phenomena. Some of the thirds that are the product of the couple's interpersonal and interpsychic relations have been discussed more fully in Chapters 3 and 4. The term "interpsychic" refers to the joint functioning and mutual influence of two psyches on one another (Bolognini, 2004).

From the link perspective, the third is the link itself that is inevitably created in a relationship between two or more. A third entity, which is not simply the aggregate of the two psyches but new and not predetermined, is created by the couple, and this entity, the link, once created, influences and shapes the couple. This has been described by Julio Moreno,

> This production is not a mere externalisation of the internal contents of the linked subjects, but a new production. In this way, the link, any link, is not the result of the algebraic sum of the contents of the psychic apparatuses involved (including the conscious and the unconscious) or of the transfer of information from one participant to the other. What characterises the link is the development in the virtual spaces in between participants surpluses and emergents that did not exist before the encounter.
>
> (Moreno, 2014, p. 4, cited in Kleiman, 2016)

DOI: 10.4324/9781003352518-7

Within the Tavistock and other object relations approaches, there are different kinds of thirds, one of which is the coming together of a couple's shared anxieties, such as their co-constructed shared phantasies (Bannister & Pincus, 1965) or their unconscious beliefs (Britton, 1998; Morgan 2010) and the shared defences they establish to mediate them (see Chapter 4). Dicks' concept of a joint marital personality (Dicks, 1967/1993) and the creation of the couple's projective system also refer to defensive and developmental systems a couple create between them that influence the way they interact. Or the third entity may be a shared value system that the couple create between them, as in Kernberg's concept of a couple superego (Kernberg, 1993). These kinds of thirds have a structuring function for the relationship, and what they share with the link perspective is that once created they influence the couple's relating. One can also think of these thirds as interrelated, in that a dynamic system of shared anxieties, phantasies and beliefs generate a shared defensive system, which in turn can result in a shared value system.

Other kinds of third, mainly within the Tavistock approach, are those that function in a relationship as a symbolic entity and stem from psychic developments within the couple, fostering containment, reflective space and creativity. Examples here are the marriage or relationship as a psychological container (Colman, 1993), the reflective space found in the marital triangle (Ruszczynski, 2005) or the development of a couple state of mind (Morgan, 2001, 2019) and creative couple (Morgan, 2005).

Before further elaborating these thirds developed within the context of psychoanalytic couple relations, I will touch on some relevant concepts from the broader analytic field.

The analytic third

Thomas Ogden's (2004) concept of the analytic third describes the link jointly built by the interaction of analyst and patient that is specific to each analytic pair, and which in turn feeds the internal experience of both. He extends and elaborates Winnicott's notion that "There is no such thing as an infant [apart from the maternal provision] (Winnicott, 1960, p. 39)", meaning that the infant only exists within the context of the maternal provision. Describing this in the context of the relationship between analyst and analysand, he says

"This third subjectivity, the intersubjective analytic third", is the product of a unique dialectic generated by/between the separate subjectivities of analyst and analysand within the analytic setting. It is a subjectivity that seems to take on a life of its own in the interpersonal field, generated between analyst and analysand (Ogden, 2004, p. 169).

The analytic third can be transposed onto other relationships between two and has similarities with the link perspective. These concepts share the idea that the individual exists simultaneously in the interpsychic and the intrapsychic. It is not about separating out the members of the link but seeing that they always exist within it.

Transitional space

Following Winnicott (1971), the idea of a transitional area of potential space between a couple has been explored in some recent publications (Friend, 2013, 2021; Joyce, 2019; Hewison, 2023). In his account of early development, Winnicott describes an intermediate area of transitional space which is neither just the infant's psychic reality nor external reality. This illusory area of play and creativity comes prior to the infant being able to recognise the mother or primary carer as separate from himself, and for Winnicott it was important that this didn't happen prematurely. Mature love in couple relations tends to be seen as following a relinquishment of the illusory state, in favour of relating that involves among other things the recognition of the other as separate. However, some have argued that this illusory state is important even within a mature love relationship.

According to Angela Joyce

as a couple relationship gets established, there are regressive pulls to the illusory state of merger and one-ness, which might be dangerous if in the two individuals this is predicated on the collapse of the paradox that allowed the illusion to be experienced originally. This is the paradox of one-ness and two-ness, with mother and infant as one, although, in objective reality, they are two. I would say that this collapse *is* the state of disintegration, a disaster that heralds the possibility of annihilation and ushers defences with which to fend off this catastrophe. This is not the same as un-integration, which is a creative, generative state of possibilities.

(Joyce, 2019, p. 161)

To be able to return to states of illusory un-integration rather than disintegration in an adult couple relationship, Joyce points out that there needs to be a sufficient sense of safety to contain this regression. Friend also explores these regressive and potentially creative states in couple relations. She believes that even in more mature love illusion remains including the aspects of idealisation, fantasy and merged boundaries (Friend, 2013)

Friend argues for supporting couples in being able to, "hold a tension between more mature, reasoned kinds of relating on the one hand, with the creative potential of less rational, more aesthetic qualities of relating to the other" (Friend, 2013, p. 5).

These ideas challenge an understanding of mature love based solely on depressive position capacities such as coming to terms with the separateness of the other, recognising their good and bad aspects (and one's own) and having concern and gratitude for the other. It is argued by these writers that within mature love there can be regression to illusory states, which if existing within the context of mature love and security can be creative for the couple.

A third position

Britton saw a third position as a development that occurs as the child comes to terms with the Oedipal situation. In a much-cited description, he writes:

If the link between the parents perceived in love and hate can be tolerated in the child's mind, it provides him with the prototype for an object relationship of a third kind in which he is a witness and not a participant. A third position then comes into existence from which object relationships can be observed. Given this, we can also envisage being observed. This provides us with a capacity for seeing ourselves in interaction with others and for entertaining another point of view whilst retaining our own, for reflecting on ourselves whilst being ourselves.

(Britton, 1989, p. 87)

This conceptualisation has been very influential to theorising analytic work with couples; for example, in the concept of a couple state of mind and the marital triangle as elaborated below.

Couple perspectives – The link

Fundamental to the link perspective is the idea that the link is created by the conjunction of the two members of the couple and once established constitutes them. Nicolò and Norsa describe this aspect of the link in the following way:

Once constructed, it takes on a life of its own, independent from the subjects, able to influence them, and constituting a third element, a new entity affecting the functioning of the family and couple, acting on the context and on the members who produced it.

(Nicolò & Norsa, 2017, p. 29)

And Pickering, from an object relations/Jungian perspective also observes,

There are the two partners, the complex networks and dynamics of relations between them and the relationship itself, which creates a fluid, interpenetrating and interacting field, the intersubjective marital third. This is revealed by the communication of the individuals, but controlled by neither.

(Pickering, 2008, p. 143)

The contribution of link theory provides a particular discourse which puts the creation of something "new" as an outcome of the couple's relating centre stage. The members of the couple come together with their separate histories, cultures, developmental experiences, beliefs and values and a third is created which is specific and unique to their bond. The third is not an aggregate of the two individuals but the creation of a new entity which exists only in their link and did not exist prior to it. The link, on being constituted, now invests the couple so that they become subjects of the link.

Couple perspectives – The Tavistock and other object relations approaches

The couple's projective system and joint marital personality

The couple projective system is a defensive and potentially developmental third entity co-created by the couple. Bannister and Pincus described a couple's projective system in the following way:

> Into marriage each partner brings conscious and unconscious drives, attitudes and needs which are partly acceptable and partly unacceptable to himself. Those attitudes or drives which each has difficulty in accepting in himself, each might try to attribute to a partner. The more at war with himself an individual is, the more of himself he may project, and the more dependent he may become on the container of his projections. In marriage, the relationship with the partner who is thus invaded then partly becomes a relationship with oneself, and the partner ceases to exist as an individual in his own right.
>
> (Bannister & Pincus, 1965, pp. 61–62)

Dicks hypothesised that there was an "unconscious complementariness" between the individuals in a couple, in which they divided up between them different aspects of themselves but together they created a whole – a joint marital personality. He saw that there were "unconscious forces which flow between the partner forming bonds of a 'positive' and 'negative kind', a love-hate involvement". This, he believed, was true for all couples, and as in the link perspective, each couple was "an integrate different from the mere sum of its parts" (Dicks, 1967/1993, p. 8).

This process, occurring through mutual projective identification, could over time enable each partner to re-introject these split off parts of the self, leading to growth in the individual and the relationship. As Scharff describes,

> the well-functioning, maturing projective identificatory system enables the person to take back impoverishing projections. It simultaneously enriches the self and maximises concern for the spouse as a separate person, as well as refurbishing the internal object or part of the self to which the spouse corresponds.
>
> (Scharff, 1992, p. 138)

Selfdyad

Richard Zeitner re-conceptualised Dicks' joint marital personality by drawing on the thinking of Heinz Kohut's self-psychology approach and coined the term "selfdyad". A selfdyad is a conjoint entity in which an important aspect of each partner's self finds a complementary aspect in the other. A third is created in that there is now a "conjoint entity, which hereafter will be different from the two individuals comprising it" (2016, p. 8).

According to Zeitner,

> For the relationship to remain loving and resilient, the selfdyad must continue to provide selfobject relatedness as a kind of interpersonal nourishment, while supporting and affirming both partners' psychic contributions to the selfdyad – through variations of mirroring, idealising, and twinship – Kohut's triad of selfobject functions (Kohut, 1971, 1977).

Zeitner believes that for the relationship to remain vital through the couple's life cycle the selfdyad must continue to nourish the individuals through growth, change and regression.

Couples in collusion

A similar idea to that of a joint marital personality was described by Willi, in terms of a couple's collusion (see Chapter 3). He saw that marital relations were often founded on shared themes that were both fascinating and disturbing and drew the couple together. In order to manage their shared anxieties, couples create a defensive system in which each carry opposite aspects of a shared theme or issue. They then can act out these central intrapsychic conflicts in a polarised way.

Joint couple superego and joint ego ideal

Otto Kernberg postulates that in couple relations the members of the couple develop a joint superego which also takes on an identity of its own.

> Just as the couple becomes the repository of both partners' conscious and unconscious sexual fantasies and desires, and of their consciously and unconsciously activated internalized object relations, so does the couple activate both partners' conscious and unconscious superego functions. It also, I suggest, constitutes a potential new superego system of its own.
>
> (Kernberg, 1993, p. 653)

The way in which this new joint superego functions depends on its nature, which stems from the nature of each partner's superego. If the joint superego is primitive, it may threaten the capacity for sexual love and have other destructive impacts on the relationship. However, if there is a mature joint superego in which there is concern for the self and the other, it fosters love and commitment and protects and supports the couple's relations in many ways, including in being able to be creative in resolving conflict. Kernberg also describes the couple's development of a joint ego ideal, which becomes established by the couple over time, and which enables the couple to continue to develop and manage pressures on the relationship:

> To be dedicated to a love relationship as a life project that infiltrates the tasks of every day is another major, perhaps the most essential aspect of a love relationship – the counterpart to the capacity for an ongoing, enlivening and exciting

interest in the personality and the subjective experience of the other. It is an expression of the 'joint ego ideal' established by the couple throughout time, the basis for ongoing work on the relationship, and for the protection of its boundaries and of its survival under adversity (Kernberg, 1995).

(Kernberg, 2011, p. 1507)

The relational third

In a couple relationship, there is a way in which the coming together of two individuals gives rise to a third form of subjectivity, which emerges through their coupling. A 'couple' contains the two individuals, each with their separate personality, but there is a sense of a third presence circling around the two partners, revealed (or concealed) by the communications of the individuals, but controlled by neither. I call this 'the relational third' (Pickering, 2006, 2008).

(Pickering, 2011, p. 55)

An aspect of this third presence may be in the form of shared unprocessed traumatic experiences in the partners' childhoods or carried from previous generations. Often residing deeply in the unconscious of each partner, they may have an unseen presence in the relationship. Pickering uses the evocative terms "malignant dowry" to capture the unresolved traumatic experiences brought into the relationship and then taking residence there as a "malignant third". The malignant third can grip the couple's relationship and create between them an "interlocking traumatic scene" (Pickering, 2011, p. 52).

Shared unconscious phantasy

In the Tavistock approach, unconscious phantasy was one of several psychoanalytic concepts to be re-conceptualised in terms of a couple's unconscious relations. The concept of shared unconscious phantasy (Bannister & Pincus, 1965) describes a dovetailing of each partner's unconscious phantasies and their ways of seeing the world along with concomitant anxieties. These unconscious phantasies were seen as an element in the unconscious choice of partner and something that could be dissipated in the reality testing contact with an other, or strengthened where they met something similar in the partner. The shared unconscious phantasies generated defensive systems in the couple which then had a structuring effect on the relationship.

Unconscious beliefs about being a couple

In his book *Belief and Imagination*, Britton (1998) puts forward the idea that some unconscious phantasies reside in the unconscious as facts and are not amenable to change through contact with external reality. As described in Chapter 4, such beliefs are also described in a similar way by Storr as delusions. Following Storr and Britton, one might therefore differentiate between shared unconscious phantasy and unconscious beliefs based on their relation to reality. Shared unconscious phantasy remains potentially open to alteration in the light of reality and the process of taking in non-confirmatory experience. Unconscious beliefs replace curiosity with certainty and impair the capacity for thinking.

As well as conscious beliefs about what a couple is and fantasies about what the pair may aspire to be, there are often deeply held unconscious beliefs about the meaning of relating and being part of a couple which do not get tested out against reality. The beliefs can be shared beliefs that form a hidden backdrop to the couple's relationship, influencing the couples relating and their perception of their relationship (Morgan, 2010).

Marriage as psychological container

Developing an idea embedded in the Tavistock approach of an intimate couple relationship being potentially therapeutic, Colman conceived of the relationship itself as having a containing function for the partners within it. He made the conceptual shift from the idea of each partner containing the other through a reciprocal developmental projective system that they create, to the idea of the relationship itself as a symbolic psychological container, which contains both members of the couple.

The relationship itself becomes the container, the creative outcome of the couple's union, to which both partners can relate. It
is an image of something the couple are continually in the process of creating, sustaining, and maintaining, while at the same
time feeling that they exist within it – are contained by it.

(Colman, 1993, pp. 89–90)

For the relationship to function as a container, it needs to have
several qualities. Colman argued it has to be flexible enough to
support the inevitable transitions in a couple's life, stable enough
to protect them from the anxieties that are generated by change,
and to be boundaried, consisting of a shared private space which
excludes others.

The marital triangle

Ruszczynski's (2005) concept of the marital triangle draws on
Britton's idea of triangular space as an outcome of the Oedipal
situation. As described above, Britton elucidated how the infant's
developing awareness of the relationship between the parental
couple leads to the creation of a different kind of space – a triangular space. The infant can then observe a couple or be part of a
couple observed by a third. This development opens psychic
space, and most significantly, as Britton describes, "this provides
us with a capacity for seeing ourselves in interaction with others
and for entertaining another point of view whilst retaining our
own, for reflecting on ourselves whilst being ourselves" (Britton,
1989, p. 87).

Ruszczynski thought about this dynamic as it occurs later in
life, when forming an adult couple relationship. The marital triangle comes into being when the two individuals conceive of their
relationship as a symbolic third which has a dynamic identity of
its own. An important aspect of the marital triangle is that of
space and symmetry, in which there can be movement and a more
or less equal consideration between the needs of each partner and
of the relationship. The space between the elements of the triangle
promotes a reflective capacity in the relationship. Evidence that a
marital triangle has been developed within a relationship is seen

when an actual third – for example, a child, work, or extended family – impacts on the couple and if the needs of this "third" can be balanced with the needs of the other members of the triangle.

A couple state of mind

A couple state of mind builds on the idea of the couple or the relationship as the patient and what is created between them, a view intrinsic to the Tavistock model and most psychoanalytic approaches to couple relations. The concept of a couple state of mind was developed by Morgan (2001, 2019) to encompass the therapeutic stance of the couple analyst and the internalisation by the couple of a couple state of mind as an aim of the therapeutic process.

The concept also builds on the idea that Britton formulated in relation to the Oedipal situation. It is a psychic development in which the partners in a relationship can move from being subjectively involved in their relationship to being able to stand outside it and observe and reflect upon what they are creating together. It is a capacity to be both psychologically inside and outside the relationship. This is a move from a two-person interaction, which in conflictual situations can have the emotional quality of "what you are doing to me or not doing for me". Instead, a triangular space is created, in which it is possible to step outside the relationship and from a third position observe "what we are doing to, or not doing for, each other", and further "what we might be creating together".

For some people, there is a natural developmental trajectory towards a couple state of mind. For others there is a tendency to see things only from the two-person perspective of how the other impinges upon or meets the needs of the self. With the development of a couple state of mind, the couple have a valuable tool which enables them, when needed, to be able to reflect on their relationship and what they are creating together and to recover from interactions which have broken down into a form of two-person relating.

The following is an illustration of a couple beginning to develop a couple state of mind.

Clinical example: Abby and Elish

Abby and Elish had been in couple therapy for just over a year. They came for therapy because they had very heated arguments which were hard to recover from. The arguments were often about their children – they had different parenting styles, which they found hard to reconcile. When most anxious about the children, they blamed each other. In one session, they reported an argument about one of their daughters, Ella (age 12), who they agreed was spending too much time on social media. They had another daughter Rosa, almost two. Their anxiety was related to her falling behind with schoolwork, her difficulties with friendships as well as the content she might be accessing. Abby blamed Elish for not keeping an eye on Ella's phone usage. Elish was furious as she felt it was impossible to keep on top of this while also attending to their two-year-old when Abby was at work. She felt all her efforts went unrecognised by Abby.

Abby reflected on how the arguments between them always felt familiar, and Elish agreed with a deep sigh. They then talked about how they both felt Ella got overlooked because Rosa needed so much attention. Without too much blaming, Abby talked about how she felt Elish could be too soft with Ella, and Elish felt that sometimes Abby was too harsh and controlling. Abby said that Elish letting Ella get away with things brings out a controlling, critical part of her, and she doesn't like it. "It's really hard for us to get this right with Ella", Abby exclaimed.

This is a very typical exchange between a couple who are anxious about their children, have little time together and are often tired. Anxiety is managed by verbal exchanges in which each tries to rid themself of their own anxieties and project them into the other, who is seen as being to blame. They were familiar with this dynamic and so was the therapist. However, what felt different was that on this occasion they were able to find a third position in which they could reflect on what they were creating between them. This capacity marked the beginning of a much needed resource in their relationship, a couple state of mind.

The creative couple

A further development of a couple state of mind is the creative couple capacity (Morgan, 2005). In being able to take a third position in which it is possible to observe their own relating, there is a movement for each partner in the couple from their subjective experience to a more reflective objective position, in which two different thoughts or viewpoints can be encountered.

If there is a capacity in each partner for tolerating difference and otherness, then it might be possible to allow the differences to mate. This process requires being able to allow previous preconceptions to break down, despite not knowing what may be newly created. This capacity to allow two psyches to come together and mate without any kind of predetermined outcome is the creative couple function. With the development of a creative couple capacity, the couple can experience their relationship as a resource, the whole being greater than the sum of the parts.

The creative couple function is something that even a couple with this capacity move in and out of. In fact, it can be quite hard to get into this place, and the couple can't function like this all the time. As stated above, difference and otherness are not easy to encounter, and instead of opening one's mind to this, there may be a wish to avoid it (see Chapter 5). It is through the activity of curiosity and the capacity to entertain different points of view that one can maintain an open mind and bear not knowing until something new emerges. However, as Puget pointed out, we find uncertainty difficult (Puget, 2010).

In summary, there are various descriptions of the unconscious creation of a couple by two people in an intimate relationship. This is considered an entity separate to the two individuals who have unconsciously created it, as in the Gestalt expression "the whole is greater than the sum of its parts". In addition to this, the therapeutic task as conceived of in the Tavistock model can be seen as enabling the two individuals to create for themselves a separate space, a third position in their imagination from which they can discover and observe the "in between" of their couple relating.

References

Bannister, K. & Pincus, L. (1965). *Shared Phantasy in Marital Problems: Therapy in a Four-Person Relationship.* London: Institute of Marital Studies.

Bolognini, S. (2004). Intrapsychic-interpsychic. *International Journal of Psychoanalysis*, 85: 337–358.

Britton, R. (1989). The missing link: Parental sexuality in the Oedipus Complex. In: J. Steiner (Ed.), *The Oedipus Complex Today: Clinical Implications* (pp. 83–101). London: Karnac.

Britton, R. (1998). Belief and psychic reality. In: R. Britton, *Belief and Imagination: Explorations in Psychoanalysis* (pp. 8–18). London: Routledge.

Colman, W. (1993). Marriage as a psychological container. In: S. Ruszczynski (Ed.), *Psychotherapy with Couples: Theory and Practice at the Tavistock Institute of Marital Studies* (pp. 70–96). London: Karnac.

Dicks, H. V. (1967/1993). *Marital Tensions. Clinical Studies towards a Psychological Theory of Interaction.* London: Karnac.

Friend, J. (2013). Love as a creative illusion and its place in psychoanalytic couple psychotherapy. *Couple and Family Psychoanalysis*, 3 (1): 3–14.

Friend, J. (2021). Creative illusion in couples: thoughts about the value of transitional experience for couple relationships. *Couple and Family Psychoanalysis*, 11 (2): 158–169. London: Phoenix.

Hewison, D. (2023). Re-visioning creativity in couple psychanalysis: the importance of Winnicott and Bollas in clinical practice. In: S. Nathans (Ed.), *More about Couples on the Couch: Approaching Psychoanalytic Couple Psychotherapy from an Expanded Perspective.* London & New York: Routledge.

Joyce, A. (2019). The couple, the self, and the problem of the other. *Couple and Family Psychoanalysis*, 9: 154–166.

Kernberg, O. F. (1993). The couple's constructive and destructive superego functions. *Journal of the American Psychoanalytic Association*, 41: 653–677.

Kernberg, O. F. (2011). Limitations to the capacity to love. *International Journal of Psycho-Analysis*, 92: 1501–1515.

Kleiman, S. (2016). The links: What is produced in the space between others. *Couple and Family Psychoanalysis*, 6 (2): 173–180.

Morgan, M. (2001). First contacts: The therapist's "couple state of mind" as a factor in the containment of couples seen for initial consultations. In: F. Grier (Ed.), *Brief Encounters with Couples* (pp. 17–32). London: Karnac.

Morgan, M. (2005). On being able to be a couple: The importance of a "creative couple" in psychic life. In: F. Grier (Ed.), *Oedipus and the Couple* (pp. 9–30). London: Karnac.

Morgan, M. (2010). Unconscious beliefs about being a couple. *Fort Da*, 16 (1): 36–55.

Morgan, M. (2019). *A Couple State of Mind: Psychoanalysis of Couples and the Tavistock Relationships Model*. London & New York: Routledge.

Nicolò, A.M. & Norsa, D. (2017). Brief introductions to theoretical and clinical approaches around the world. In D. E. Scharff & E. Palacios (Eds.), *Family and Couple Psychoanalysis: A Global Perspective* (pp. 27–33). London: Karnac.

Ogden, T. (1994). *Subjects of Analysis*. Northvale, NJ: Jason Aronson.

Ogden, T. H. (2004). The analytic third: Implications for psychoanalytic theory and technique. *Psychoanalytic Quarterly*, 73: 167–195.

Pickering, J. (2008). *Being in Love: Therapeutic Pathways through Psychological Obstacles to Love*. London & New York: Routledge.

Pickering, J. (2011). Bion and the couple. *Couple and Family Psychoanalysis*, 1 (1): 49–68. London: Karnac.

Puget, J. (2010). The subjectivity of certainty and the subjectivity of uncertainty. *Psychoanalytic Dialogues*, 20: 4–20.

Ruszczynski, S. (2005). Reflective space in the intimate couple relationship: The marital triangle. In: F. Grier (Ed.), *Oedipus and the Couple* (pp. 31–47). London: Karnac.

Scharff, J. S. (1992). Projective and introjective identification, love and the internal couple. In: J. Scharff, *Projective and Introjective Identification and the Use of the Therapist's Self* (pp. 133–157). New Jersey & London: Jason Aronson.

Winnicott, D. W. (1971). Transitional objects and transitional phenomena. In *Playing and Reality* (pp. 1–125). New York: Basic Books.

Zeitner, R. (2012). *Self Within Marriage: The Foundation for Lasting Relationships*. New York: Routledge.

Zeitner, R. M. (2016). Implications of the intergenerational linking functions for the parental selfdyad in the treatment of a narcissistic adolescent. *Couple and Family Psychoanalysis*, 6: 7–24.

Chapter 7

Sex and sexuality in couple relations

Sexuality is a psychological, relational, biological and neurological phenomenon. It is an intrinsic part of adult intimate relations, encompassing each partner's biological sex, gender identification, sexual identity and sexual orientation, and all these elements have specific meanings for the individual. Some of these elements of sexuality are formed over time as part of the individual's psychosexual development. In an intimate adult relationship, the self and the other's sexuality meet and become part of the couple's intimate bond.

Gender identity, particularly where the experience of the physical sexual body is not aligned with the gendered experience of self, is a prominent issue in some contemporary western societies. Transsexuality may take many forms and range from experimenting with cross dressing, to surgery to change the body. There may also be a wish not to be constrained by being one gender or by being gendered, with the individual identifying as non-binary. For young adults, there is often experimentation with gender, sexual identity and orientation in the process of working out one's sexuality. Queer theory resists the categorisation of sex, gender and sexuality. Robinson and Kentridge see "queerness" as a language which might assert "an expanded set of sexual practices, relationship structures or ways of expressing or subverting gender" (2022, p. 107).

The way sexuality is expressed is affected by wider cultural and societal norms and constraints. For example, what it means to be male or female in one culture may be very different in another. In some western societies, same sex couples with children are more

DOI: 10.4324/9781003352518-8

normative, while in others it is prohibited. There is more scope in some cultures than in others for young people to experiment as part of their development with sexual identity and sexual orientation. Importantly, "sex" also refers to the physical, emotional and psychological sexual relations a couple create between them, including an absence of sex.

In this chapter, I will explore some areas of contemporary psychoanalytic thinking in sex and sexuality that seem particularly relevant to couple relations:

1) Sexual desire and loss of desire in heterosexual and same sex relationships
2) Internalised homophobia
3) The structuring of sexual relations – from monogamous to polyamorous
4) The impact of social media and pornography on young people's development of their sexuality

This will of necessity omit a great deal, but for a fuller account of contemporary couple psychoanalytic thinking in this area, I would recommend Clulow, *Sex, Attachment and Couple Psychotherapy* (2009), Hertzmann and Newbigin, *Sexuality and Gender Now* (2020) and McCann, *Same-Sex Couples and other Identities* (2022).

1) Desire

The nature of sexual desire and the perplexing problem of loss of desire has drawn the attention of psychoanalysts from the individual and couple fields. It has been understood through several lenses; for example, neurobiology, the absence of the mirroring of infantile sexuality, the different drives of sex and attachment, the core complex, and the psychological elements of aggression and transgression present in sexual relations.

Sexual desire very often fuels the process of two people forming an intimate relationship. All the complexities of sexuality come into play – the biological need to mate and reproduce, the neurological and psychological components contributing to falling in love, the psychosexual developments leading to the young person being ready for adult intimacy. Many couples describe an exciting and fulfilling sex life at the beginning of their relationship, and many also find that this dissipates later. There are several ways in which this has been understood.

Neuroscience

Discoveries in neuroscience have shown that in the brain there are different and opposing systems driving attachment to that of sexual desire. Specific areas of the brain are activated in the early "in-love" stage of couple relations. The hormones oestrogen and testosterone secrete oxytocin and vasopressin, which underpin lust, whilst other areas of the brain are deactivated – for example, the prefrontal cortex, which gives us the ability to assess and think clearly. Janice Hiller, exploring the activity of the brain in relation to sexual desire notes that,

> Due to the separate activation of lust, romantic attraction, and attachment, humans have developed a range of reproductive strategies and mating behaviours that promote the maintenance of loving bonds but can also lead to intense disappointment and pain if hopes and desires are not fulfilled.
>
> (Hiller, 2024, p. 23)

Hiller shows that once the couple become securely attached other areas of the brain come into play and desire lessens. This is not the whole story, but it is interesting that these changes in the brain correspond, at least for some couples, with the changes they experience in levels of sexual desire.

Enigma, mirroring and attachment

Ruth Stein (2008) and Mary Target (2007) developed some of the thinking of Laplanche, exploring the enigmatic nature of sexuality. They have suggested that because the developing infant's sexuality cannot be mirrored accurately by the mother or primary caregiver in the way that other feelings can potentially be, there remains something unknowable and enigmatic in one's sexuality, an incongruence within the self which is then associated with sexual feelings and calls out to be elaborated by another.

> Incongruent mirroring disrupts self-coherence, generating a sense of pressure and contradiction in relation to the psychosexual. The aroused baby interprets the mother's responses as a mirror of his own experience and identifies them as his own, but since they are not mirrored 'contingently' (in a manner faithful to his own affects and experiences), they are simultaneously experienced as not his own, as alien.
>
> (Target, 2007, p. 523)

It is argued that this mirroring is only found later in adult life through a sexual relationship with another. Then in long-term, securely attached relationships the enigmatic nature of sexual relating dissipates; sexuality is more integrated into the self but sexual desire decreases.

This theory about sexuality makes sense of the biological imperative to partner and have sex, and once one has procreated for this need to diminish. However, it might be questioned as to whether our sexuality is ever completely mirrored by another and known by us. A sexual relationship requires the couple to bear the transient nature of sexuality; what was exciting once may, with familiarity, be less so now. There might be changing levels of sexual desire along with changing bodies. The meaning of sex for the partners in a relationship may become less aligned. A sexual relationship has to be re-found and reconfigured over time, involving loss, change and potentially new discoveries.

The core complex

Another relevant psychoanalytic concept in relation to desire and loss of desire is that of the "core complex" (Glasser, 1979). The core complex is conceptualised as a dynamic between the infant and the mother or primary carer in which the infant's intense desire for the mother and a wish to merge with her creates a claustrophobic anxiety of engulfment in the infant. The infant then withdraws from the mother or primary carer to preserve the self, but this leads to another anxiety about abandonment and thus closeness is sought again.

This dynamic between closeness and merger and distancing and abandonment continues inevitably in later relationships and is part of what a couple has to manage in their intimate relating, albeit not usually in such an intense or extreme oscillatory dynamic. Merging at the beginning of a relationship might feel to be pleasurable, resonating with early undifferentiated states in relation to the primary object, only to later become suffocating at least for one partner. For some individuals, perhaps more often men, sex can be a way of creating or re-finding intimacy, and they sometimes can express an intensity of need which the female partner finds claustrophobic, too needy and childlike. For others, more often women, emotional intimacy is an important prequel to sex.

Sexual excitement can also be thought of as a being on the cusp of separateness and oneness. Kernberg, for example, states that the two crucial features of sexual love are, "The firm boundaries of the self and the constant awareness of the indissoluble separateness of individuals, on the one hand, and the sense of transcendence, of becoming one with the loved person, on the other" (Kernberg, 1995, p. 43).

Newbigin also captures this paradox in sexual relations: "while sexual intimacy involves identifying with the other's pleasure, it also, simultaneously, involves a release of the requirement to keep the other in mind, in favour of a letting go in pursuit of one's own climax" (Newbigin, 2020, p. 26).

These elements of sexual desire – the identification with the other's desire, the need to ruthlessly pursue one's own desire and managing being both one and separate – highlight just some of the paradoxes and complexities of sexual experience. It is also clear that sexual desire is not a discreet entity in that it can also contain elements of primitive and sometimes unmet needs.

Sex, aggression and transgression

Other psychoanalysts have linked sexual desire or, specifically, sexual excitement with aggression and transgression. Entering another body through penetration and the engulfment of the other involve aggression, and sexual fantasies often involve aggression (Freud, 1919; Kahr, 2007).

Robert Stoller argued there is a hostility involved in sexual excitement which he felt was an attempt to undo childhood traumas and frustrations that had threatened one's masculinity or femininity (Stoller, 1979). Kernberg also thought that in sex one is working through earlier developmental experiences. For him, transgression includes a feeling of triumph over the Oedipal couple, and becoming oneself part of the sexual couple fosters erotic desire. Aggression is there too:

> Erotic desire includes a sense that the object is both offering and withholding itself, and sexual penetration or engulfing the object is a violation of the other's boundaries. In this sense, transgression involves aggression against the object as well, aggression that is exciting in its pleasurable gratification, reverberating with the capacity to experience pleasure in pain and projecting that capacity onto the other. The aggression is also pleasurable because it is contained by a loving relationship.
>
> (Kernberg, 1995, p. 24)

However, while aggression and transgression may be a part of adult sexuality, aggression within a couple sexual relationship needs to be linked up with loving impulses, otherwise sexual relations can go badly wrong.

David Hewison's formulation addresses this balance between love and aggression:

> Where aggression is missing, erotic satisfaction is stunted or impossible. Where aggression is used in the service of love, to get through to someone, to connect by deliberately (and rapturously) breaching the boundaries of personal space and body surface in sex, relationship has the potential to be deepened through mutual satisfying of erotic needs. Where aggression is paramount, eroticism is curtailed and becomes routine; connection between the couple is limited to acts and roles, boundaries (emotional and physical) are turned into objects to be used, or used by, and love dies.
>
> (Hewison, 2009, p. 166)

If we accept these views that sexuality stirs up earlier psychological experiences, primitive feelings of engulfment, traumatic experiences, anxieties about one's masculinity or femininity, Oedipal rivalry and more, then we can see how complex the physical act of sex can be at a deeper level. Newbigin argues that psychoanalysis has tended to downplay that which is "unruly, excessive, and aggressive in sexual experience, in pursuit of a more domesticated fantasy of a 'healthy' sexuality that is 'non-perverse', loving and properly practiced in the context of stable relationships" (2020, p. 25). Sex is unruly and takes many forms and perhaps can only be considered perverse if it is not bounded sufficiently by recognition of, and concern for, the other.

An interesting hypothesis in relation to desire and loss of desire in lesbian relationships has been put forward by Hertzmann, who suggests that for some lesbian couples there is an initial state of perfect harmony through the phantasy of the re-creation of the exclusive bond with the mother in early childhood, but one that includes sexual desire. As reality intervenes and the phantasy cannot be maintained, there is a painful loss which can be hard to recover from. "A wonderfully intense initial encounter as a couple, perhaps even lasting some time, comes to an end, the relationship takes on a different character, and sexual desire becomes problematic for one or both partners" (Hertzmann, 2020, p. 90).

In the merger with the attuned other, the only drive that links the two is a loving drive. It may be that the exclusion of both aggression and the awareness of difference kills off desire.

2) Internalised homophobia in same sex relationships

While in western cultures gay and lesbian couple relations have become more normative, including having children through IVF, egg and sperm donors, surrogacy or adoption, being in a same sex couple still has its specific challenges. Despite changes in society, it can still attract stigma. As well as experiencing homophobia from society at large, gay and lesbian couples can also struggle with an internal sense of being "not right", and this can affect their functioning as a creative couple. This has been conceptualised as internalised homophobia, which Paul Rohleder describes in the following way: "Internalised homophobia refers to feelings of self-hatred and shame among some gay men and lesbian women, arising from the introjection of negative and hostile responses from significant and important others – including social messages" (Rohleder, 2020, p. 50).

Hertzmann has developed this concept by drawing on the work of Kernberg, who posits that there is, in couple relations, a couple superego which can be constructive or destructive (Kernberg, 1993 and see also Chapter 6). She suggests "internalized homophobia, functioning as an unconscious introject, acts as host for aggressive aspects of the superego potentially resulting in a very punitive attitude towards the homosexuality of the self and of others" (Hertzmann, 2011, p. 350). In this situation, as Moss points out, "one hates oneself for wanting what one wants, and therefore, for being what one is" (Moss, 2002, p. 30).

Internalised homophobia has a detrimental affect not only on the individual's sexuality and belief in themself but also, she believes, the couple's sexual relationship and their capacity to sustain their relationship. Internalised homophobia can dampen sexual desire between a couple, as feelings of shame, depression and having little value can lead to inexplicable arguments stemming from self-hatred, which is directed towards the other. It can also contribute to aggression and violent behaviour in a couple (Renzetti, 1992 and see also Chapter 8).

Clinical example: Jim and Eric

Jim and Eric came for therapy six months after moving in together, as they found that their previously enjoyable sexual relationship was now dissipating. Before moving in together, they had engaged in an open relationship, in which each separately sought sex with others, but they decided that in moving in together they would try monogamy. Although on the whole sex with others had been fun, it had at times felt hard to negotiate between them. There had been one sexual encounter that became quite involved for Eric, and Jim had asked him to end it, which had not been easy for Eric. This had alarmed them both. As well as the loss of desire, they also felt they were quarrelling too much of the time. Their therapist was impressed with the array of things they found to argue about and started to feel these arguments served an important function for them.

The choice to have a monogamous relationship seemed very connected to the alarm they both felt that Eric may have been falling in love with someone else. However, it began to emerge that for them monogamy was associated with heteronormativity, whereas an open relationship had unconsciously validated their sexuality. Some friends and family members even commented on how they were now a "proper couple". Whether or not these comments were heterosexist, for Jim and Eric they stirred up feelings of not being a "proper couple". The therapist understood that feelings of self-hatred and not being a "proper couple" were now manifesting in both of them.

Sometimes arguing is not a form of communication but a way of trying to project unease into the other. The irritation with the other for always doing something wrong came to be thought about as a process of mutual projection into each other of their internal sense of not being "right". This massively affected their sexual desire, as if engaging in sex together would connect them up again with the projected feelings.

3) The structuring of sexual relations – From monogamous to polyamorous

Another area of interest in contemporary couple psychoanalytic thinking is about the way relationships are configured around sexuality. In contemporary western societies, there have been changes and challenges to normative thinking about what a couple is. Many couples feel that part of being a couple requires monogamy, and in choosing to be together they give up the possibility of other relationships to commit to one other. When that relationship is breached through an affair, it is felt as a betrayal and sometimes a threat to the continuing of the relationship. Affairs mean many things and impact in different ways on the monogamous couple. Sometimes it is the end of the relationship, with or without the lover becoming the new partner, but sometimes the breach confronts the couple with difficulties they hadn't seen or had turned a blind eye to, and in time they find a new way forward together.

While open relationships were for some time thought to be more meaningful to male same sex couples, other couple relationships, including heterosexual, consider this as a choice. Some couples from the beginning, or at some point in their relationship, decide to open it up to other sexual encounters or relationships. McCann defines open relationships as "a form of dyadic couple relationship that is open to partners having sex with others, although not usually forming loving or deep attachments with anyone other than the primary partner" (McCann, 2022, p. 140).

Deciding on an open relationship or a polyamorous one may be about a rejection of the idea of monogamy as a basis for coupling, or to do with other factors such as loss of desire, or different desire, as described above. What is clear is that there are many kinds of open relationships and many faces of polyamory (Fosse, 2021). In open relationships, sexual experiences with someone outside the relationship may be transient and anonymous but may also become ongoing sexual friendships. Managing an open relationship is often not easy and, as McCann points out,

> in the same way that sexual infidelity in monogamous relationships constitutes a crisis for the couple, emotional infidelity within an open relationship may be just as devastating, since it suggests that one of the partnerships formed a strong emotional connection to a sexual partner outside of the primary relationship, thereby threatening its foundation.
>
> (McCann, 2022, pp. 140–141)

Polyamory, though only chosen by a small minority, has more of a presence in contemporary western society. The clinical research done by Fosse (2021) shows that as a phenomenon it is becoming more diffused than consolidated. She says, "Polyamory is a lifestyle; it might be a sexual orientation, and it is also a sexual and cultural movement" (p. 9).

There is no one kind of polyamory; for example, it may take the form of a central couple, or many couples, or a group in which no one is in a couple. How equalitarian polyamorous relationships are varies. Thus, some polyamorous couples have the experience of being part of more than one couple, and in others there is one primary couple. Jealousy has to be managed and is an emotion that is usually frowned upon in polyamorous relating.

These different kinds of sexual arrangements may be sought for many reasons. There may be a wish to reject heteronormativity and seek liberation from normative behaviour felt as constraining. It may be a way of enhancing the sexual and emotional relationship of the primary couple, or a solution to something that is missing in the primary relationship and so on; it is not always an easy solution.

4) Impact of social media and pornography on young people's development of their sexuality

Newbigin describes,

> Today's young people in urban environments are growing up in a very diverse world, where they are faced with a smorgasbord of identities – gay, lesbian, bisexual, queer, bi-curious and so on – in which they are encouraged to appear knowing and confident. Indeed, the trying on of different sexual and gender identities may sometimes be a means of finding an enclave to retreat into from the apparently hypersexualised world that we now inhabit.
>
> (Newbigin, 2020, p. 38)

It is also not possible to underestimate the impact of social media on the developing sexuality of young people. The presentation of idealised bodily images against which a young person judges themself at the same time as having to deal with their own changing body and nascent sexuality can be crippling for some. Online personalities can influence vulnerable young people with prescribed ways of being that take on a dynamic of certainty – "this is the way you should be" – and thinking for oneself is occluded.

Online pornography can throw young people into an adult world that is unreal in its depiction of sexual confidence, perpetual desire and a ready willingness to engage in sexual acts that they may feel overwhelmed by. It is not only that the use of porn impacts on a young person's sexual development but also on their capacity to function in a relationship in which a real other is encountered. Alessandra Lemma argues that "the work of desire"– i. e., anxieties about wanting, being dependent on another to meet that desire, and having to consider the others desire – is avoided. She says,

> Waiting for an actual other who might or might not want us is replaced by the 'pornographic other' who becomes an object that can be manipulated and where sexual arousal is unimpeded by the complexities of different desires and arousal patterns, or the consideration of another person's needs that, in turn, would require us to imaginatively identify with the other. Speed thus amplifies the likelihood that the underlying psychological process necessary to sustain positive relationships is undermined.
>
> (Lemma, 2021, p. 125)

Lemma argues that the nature of online porn can have a serious effect on the capacity to mentalize in a relationship.

> Mentalisation describes a particular facet of the human imagination: an individual's awareness of mental states in himself or herself and in other people, particularly in explaining their actions. It involves perceiving and interpreting the feelings, thoughts, beliefs and wishes that explain what people do.
>
> (Bateman & Fonagy, 2019, p. 3)

Clearly this capacity is important in couple relations and has a specific impact on sexual relations. "In a sexual context, mentalizing underpins a person's ability to imagine, for example, that no matter how strong one's personal desire for sex, this does not imply that our partner feels the same" (Lemma, 2021).

The capacity to mentalize thus helps in managing different levels of sexual desire, different preferences, and frustration and disappointment when one's own desire is thwarted.

As stated at the beginning of this chapter, sex and sexuality is a complex phenomenon for the individual and within couple relations. It is unruly and evolves and changes within the life span of the individual and within couple relations. As Grier remarks,

None of us is ever quite sorted out in the area of sex, and it is perhaps both a torment and a comfort to realise that we shall never be, that an ultimate resolution is impossible, and that never fully solving this dilemma is part of what makes us human and alive rather than god-like and dead.

(Grier, 2009, p. 46)

References

Bateman, A. & Fonagy, P. (Eds.) (2019). *Handbook of Mentalizing in Mental Health Practice*. American Psychiatric Association Publishing.

Clulow, C. (Ed.) (2009). *Sex, Attachment and Couple Psychotherapy: Psychoanalytic Perspectives*. London: Karnac.

Fosse, M. J. (2021). *The Many Faces of Polyamory: Longing and Belonging in Concurrent Relationships*. New York & London: Routledge.

Freud, S. (1919). *"A Child is being Beaten": A Contribution to the Study of the Origin of Sexual Perversions*. In: The Standard Edition of the Complete Psychological Works of Sigmund Freud, Volume 17 (1917–1919): An Infantile Neurosis and Other Works (pp. 175–204). London: Hogarth Press.

Glasser, M. (1979). Some aspects of the role of aggression in the perversions. In: I. Rosen (Ed.), *Sexual Deviations* (pp. 278–305). Oxford: Oxford University Press.

Grier, F. (2009). Lively and deathly intercourse. In: C. Clulow (Ed.), *Sex, Attachment and Couple Psychotherapy: Psychoanalytic Perspectives* (pp. 45–61). London: Karnac.

Hertzmann, L. (2011). Lesbian and gay couple relationships: When internalized homophobia gets in the way of couple creativity. *Psychoanalytic Psychotherapy*, 25: 346–360.

Hertzmann, L. (2020). Losing the internal oedipal mother and loss of sexual desire. In L. Hertzmann & J. Newbigin (Eds.), *Sexuality and Gender Now: Moving beyond Heteronormativity* (pp. 81–103). London & New York: Routledge.

Hertzmann, L. & Newbigin, J. (Eds.) (2020). *Sexuality and Gender Now: Moving beyond Heteronormativity*. London & New York: Routledge.

Hewison, D. (2009). Power vs. love in sadomasochistic relationships. In: C. Clulow (Ed.), *Sex, Attachment and Couple Psychotherapy: Psychoanalytic Perspectives* (pp. 165–184). London: Karnac.

Hiller, J. (2024). *Sex in the Brain: A Neuropsychosexual Approach to Love and Intimacy*. London: Karnac.

Kahr, B. (2007). The traumatic roots of sexual fantasy. In: B. Kahr, *Sex and the Psyche* (pp. 280–310). London: Allen Lane.

Kernberg, O. F. (1993). The couple's constructive and destructive superego functions. *Journal of the American Psychoanalytic Association*, 41 (3): 653–677.

Kernberg, O. F. (1995). *Love Relations: Normality and Pathology.* New Haven, CT: Yale University Press.

Lemma, A. (2021). Introduction – Becoming sexual in digital times: The risks and harms of online pornography. *The Psychoanalytic Study of the Child*, 74(1): 118–130.

McCann, D. (Ed.) (2022). *Same-Sex Couples and Other Identities: Psychoanalytic Perspectives.* London & New York: Routledge.

Moss, D. (2002). Internalized homophobia in men: Wanting in the first person singular, hating in the first person plural. *Psychoanalytic Quarterly*, 71: 21–50.

Newbigin, J. (2020). Sex in the consulting room. In: L. Hertzmann & J. Newbigin (Eds.), *Sexuality and Gender Now: Moving beyond Heteronormativity* (pp. 19–39). London & New York: Routledge.

Renzetti, C. M. (1992). *Violent Betrayal: Partner Abuse in Lesbian Relationships.* Newbury Park, CA: Sage Publications.

Robinson, I. & Kentridge, A. (2022). Queer relationships: unmapped intimacy. In: D. McCann (Ed.), *Same-Sex Couples and Other Identities: Psychoanalytic Perspectives.* London & New York: Routledge.

Rohleder, P. (2020). Homophobia, heteronormativity, and shame. In: L. Hertzmann & J. Newbigin (Eds.), *Sexuality and Gender Now: Moving beyond Heteronormativity.* London & New York: Routledge.

Stein, R. (2008). The otherness of sexuality: Excess. *Journal of the American Psychoanalytic Association*, 56 (1): 43–71.

Stoller, R. J. (1979). *Sexual Excitement: Dynamics of Erotic Life.* London: Karnac.

Target, M. (2007). Is our sexuality our own? A developmental model of sexuality based on early affect mirroring. *British Journal of Psychotherapy*, 23 (4): 517–530.

Chapter 8

Love, hate and creativity

In this chapter, I explore love and hate in couple relations. Several psychoanalysts have conceptualised love, for example, Ethel Spector Person (1988), Otto Kernberg (1995,), Stephen Mitchell (2002) and Judith Pickering (2008). These writers explore the problems of love as well as trying to define what it is. Overall, from a psychoanalytic perspective it is possible to think about different states of love – from the "falling in love" state or "romantic love", to a more "mature love" state. Falling in love and then being in love is usually temporary and often encompasses heightened emotional states, intense sexual feelings, merger and illusion. In mature love, there is a greater capacity for an intimacy which is combined with separateness, one that is more reality based and sometimes experienced as deep and enduring.

Aggression is a complex concept in psychoanalysis, as it is used to mean different things. However, it is considered by most as a drive that is needed for life and for development (Bott Spillius et al. 2011). Hate can take many forms, interacting with love in a healthy way or split off from love and concern for the other. The integration of love and hate can be part of creativity in couple relations, while unmitigated hatred can manifest in some forms of intimate partner violence.

Being in love

Obviously, in the state of falling in 'love', we expect to see a degree of idealization of the other person, an enchantment with the partner's physical, sexual and personality features, an

DOI: 10.4324/9781003352518-9

> interest in and respect for the other person's value systems, and an intense longing for sexual intimacy, emotional closeness, and for a meeting of the minds regarding joint ways to experience the world and relate to it (Chasseguet-Smirgel, 1973).
>
> (Kernberg, 2011, p. 1502)

This description of falling in love by Kernberg, who has also written about mature love and the limitations on the capacity to love (Kernberg, 2011), is widely recognised both within and outside psychoanalysis. Falling in love is, for many, the mechanism that enables two people to take the step of committing themselves to a relationship with one other person. While there are real aspects of the other that are fallen in love with, there is also illusion, as these real aspects are exaggerated, or other less attractive or unwanted aspects of the other are occluded.

How does this in-love state, which Freud described as "psychologically so remarkable and is the normal prototype of the psychoses" (Freud, 1913, p. 89), come into being? One of the unconscious phantasies deep in the psyche may be that of finding or "re-finding" a completely intimate connection that was experienced earlier in life with one's primary object (Freud, 1905). Even if it was not at all like this, one might yearn yet more for it to be like this now, if the perfect other can be found. While these yearnings are predominantly unconscious, their outward conscious manifestations are expressed openly in popular culture; for example, the fantasy of finding one's other half, one's soul mate or "the one", as described in Chapter 3. Most people do manage at some point to relinquish the in-love state and, to varying degrees, allow something else new and unknown, based on difference and otherness, to grow between them in the intimacy they create. As the initial idealisation drops away, the reality of the other and of the relationship is recognised with its good and bad aspects.

However, discovering the other as a "new" other, less distorted by the projections that have coloured them in the in-love state, can be challenging as well as enriching. It is also interesting to consider why development from the in-love state into a more mature and potentially deeper love is more difficult for some.

Loss and mourning

Having found the idealised relationship, some couples find it very difficult to give it up because it reverberates with the earlier loss of the primary object during the Oedipal situation. The experience of loss in the early Oedipal situation, described by Klein as being in the first months of life, is hard to fully metabolise at the time, even more so when an internal good object hasn't been sufficiently established, thus it is probably only ever partially worked through. Falling in love, the re-finding of the ideal object, and ultimate loss of it, might provide the conditions within which this earlier loss can be further worked through from a position of greater ego strength and maturity. However, for some, the relinquishment of the idealised relationship can simply rekindle the earlier raw loss, and thus the idealised relationship must be held onto.

John Steiner suggests that in mature love the couple may still continue to believe the illusion, even though they now know it is not true.

> Perhaps here, in the cradle, we find the earliest appearance of irony in our lives, which may then be established as a critical step on the path to mature love. It enables us to enjoy an illusion while remaining aware it is not quite real.
>
> (Steiner, 2024, p. 569)

But without this playful capacity between reality and illusion the development towards mature love might be curtailed. The illusory state may be returned to at different times, without the couple necessarily being aware of it; for example, following the birth of their first baby, before the reality of separateness and difference returns. Friend considers that the couple's capacity for illusion, which she distinguishes from idealisation, may also play an important role once mature love is realised. "Illusion is indispensable as a form of vitalising engagement with life, and it is often through an experience of love and merger with another that it is refreshed and re-created" (Friend, 2013, p. 12).

However, for some, the phantasy of the illusory relationship can be held onto and believed to be the reality of what the relationship should be. The belief can then become a real stumbling block, as the other never lives up to or embodies the partner's phantasy of what they need them to be, and the disappointment about this becomes a paralysing force in the relationship. Such beliefs may create anxiety about the sustainability of the relationship: "if we are not in-love (or perhaps in love in the same idealised way), there must be something wrong". It is as if there is a belief that once love has been found (or re-found), it must not be let go of. Thus, there is an ever-present market in many cultures for tips and advice about how to keep one's relationship alive and exciting, emotionally and sexually, encouraging the idea that it is possible or desirable to maintain love in the same unchanging idealised way.

The other, mature love and the depressive position

Being "in love" can feel like being "one" with the other, in knowing them from the inside. It is hard to come to terms with the fact that one can never perfectly know an other. Because of the primitive feelings that are stirred up on finding oneself part of an intimate couple, some struggle in a relationship to feel separate and allow the other to be separate from the self. Whether one can see the "other" as they are is a fundamental question in terms of how much room there is for development in the relationship. They may instead re-create in their mind a version of the "other" in their own image, or an image of another shaped by their own preconceptions. Fisher argues that it is only by engaging with the separateness of the other that genuine intimacy can occur. The alternative becomes a narcissistic form of relating (Fisher, 1999).

Another way of defending against the development of mature love is by staying in the merger. Morgan has described the formation of a "projective gridlock", a projective system in which the partners, through the process of mutual projective identification, psychically live inside one another and maintain a feeling of oneness (Morgan, 1995, see also Chapter 5). It is paradoxical, since it can look like such couples are remaining in and maintaining the in-love state. However, as Stephen Mitchell observes, "total safety, predictability, and oneness, permanently established, quickly become stultifying" (Mitchell, 2002, p. 51). In a sustained merger, the relationship doesn't develop, love and hate don't interact creatively, and curiosity is kept at bay.

Moving towards a mature love state means one is now in a relationship with someone who is "other", someone who is not, and never will be, completely known. The other has limitations on their capacity or desire to meet the needs of the subject, and in addition they have needs of their own which the subject may or may not be able or willing to meet or tolerate. The anxiety this generates may result in clinging to the merger for fear of the unknown.

As the possibility of mature love emerges, some people fear what they imagine this to be. For example, the experience of being dependent on and vulnerable with another may feel threatening. If there has not been sufficient containment or holding earlier in life, an experience of secure attachment, or if the person has suffered trauma, then they may find it very difficult to trust another. Love may feel dangerous. Loving another and being loved by another may risk hurt, rejection and abandonment. Ortal Kirson-Trilling believes that to love and be loved requires a capacity to be vulnerable and "open-heartedly laying bare who we are". This capacity, she argues, is first developed in reliable early object relations and supported throughout development. However, if the couple share the experience of early relational trauma, the partners may seek to protect themselves against love (Kirson-Trilling, 2022, p. 120). The fear of love may manifest in repetitive quarrelling as a defensive manoeuvre which protects against loving and being loved (Novakovic, 2016). Love may also be defended against by hate. John Steiner, referring to the work of Melanie Klein, describes the way in which love may be hidden within hate and grievance:

> Once we recognize that love is not simply romantic and libidinal, but carries a deep burden of sorrow, guilt, and anxiety, in relation to loved and endangered objects, we can better understand that patients may find love too painful, and will try to avoid and deflect loving feelings, sometimes by increasing hatred and grievance. This means that love is sometimes buried beneath hate, and is only released as the hate is analysed.
>
> (Steiner, 2017)

For those who have had a good enough early experience that has enabled them to develop basic trust and an internal sense of security, it feels much more possible to love and allow oneself to be loved in an ordinary and non-idealised way. Kernberg describes several elements of mature love – an ongoing curiosity and interest in the other, the presence of basic trust, mutual empathy and capacity for honesty, the capacity to forgive and ask for forgiveness (especially after aggression), and gratitude for the existence of the other person and the love received (Kernberg, 2011).

Another way of thinking about the movement from an in-love state to the mature love state is through the Kleinian lens of the paranoid schizoid and depressive position relating. Whereas mature love may be thought of as a depressive position capacity, it can also become a stagnant kind of retreat. Britton has made an essential point about the continually evolving movement between the paranoid schizoid and depressive positions and that the depressive position is not an end point. He points out that Kleinian theory, as it has developed,

> implies that the depressive position is no final resting place, that leaving the security of depressive-position coherence for a new round of fragmented, persecuting uncertainties is necessary for development. The only alternative to continuous development is regression; in a world of flux an attempt to stand still produces a retreat. Yesterday's depressive position becomes tomorrow's defensive organisation.
>
> (1998, p. 73)

Thus, the capacities that can be seen to exist in mature love are not necessarily stable and certainly not absolutes – trust, empathy, forgiveness, and curiosity may be challenging to maintain and be tested out in the relationship many times, sometimes failing. An aspect of mature love might be the awareness and acceptance of what is not working now (even though it might have before), along with the security to allow it to come apart and be re-configured between the two.

It may also be, as suggested above, that these two psychic states of love are unnecessarily polarised, and in enduring and secure enough relationships there is more fluidity between these two positions (Joyce, 2019; Friend, 2021; Hewison, 2023). For Winnicott, creativity is innate and given what he calls a "facilitating environment"; it is the process of the infant discovering his or her true self. These unintegrated dynamics between a couple may be expressed in both loving and hating ways, which if the couple exist within a secure enough relationship leads to development in the individual and the couple.

In whatever way the regression occurs – as a return to temporary states of merger, to states of hate and aggression or to unintegration in the paranoid-schizoid position – the integrated mature love state does have to come apart and be re-configured many times in the life cycle of any couple. This is because there is a danger that with familiarity in an enduring relationship curiosity recedes, and without this one is back in that earlier place of thinking one "knows" the other. One then might lose the important capacity to investigate one's own feelings and the other's, which is essential in the process of knowing about hate as well as love.

Love and hate and aggression

Freud had, in 1915, observed that the opposite of love was not hate but indifference (Freud, 1915, p. 133). Bion (1962) described the links in emotional relationships as those of L, H and K, standing for Love, Hate and the desire to Know. All of these are important in the couple relationship. The members of the couple can hate the other as well as love them, and those in relationships usually discover that these different emotions cannot be avoided. When the other frustrates and says and does things one does not like or understand and is different from the self in ways that are hard to accept, this can give rise to hatred. Mitchell argues that there are many subtle forms of hatred which are part of ordinary life and love; for example, "emotional detachment, provocative testing, strategies of control, retaliation. The most interesting crimes of passion take place only in our minds. But our minds are very important places" (Mitchell, 2002, p. 120).

Couples can feel alarmed to discover the hatred or aggression in their minds and as expressed in their relationship, and for some it goes underground. It can then be acted out in destructive behaviour or have an ongoing, insidious effect on the relationship, including their sexual relationship. In a paper on Bion's L, H and K, Grier describes work with a couple who were worried that they were becoming remote from each other and feeling anxious and that their love for each other was under threat. As he conceived of it, the couple had massive problems with H. The knowledge about "H" was a disowned and split off part of their relationship. Interpretive work on the mutual hatred he had observed in the therapy with them and their attempts to disguise it was fruitful. He says,

> to their intense surprise and relief, the result was not catastrophe, but a freeing of their capacity to love and get to know each other, which led spontaneously to their recovering sexual links in the marriage. Knowledge about H was engaged with, and this increased their desire for intellectual, emotional and sexual intercourse.
>
> (2009, p. 53)

This example illustrates what can happen in couple relations if hate and aggression are denied or avoided. Suppressed hate or unacknowledged hate may block love and liveliness, and it may also lead to a turning away from the other. Knowing about hate alongside love can lead to development in the relationship. In Kernberg's view, aggression in the life cycle of the couple is inevitable but need not be a destructive force:

> The ambivalence of all relationships implies that events of mutual aggression are unavoidable in the course of a life lived together but, by the same token, the possibility of their clarification and resolution carries with it the possibility of further strengthening and deepening the relationship.
>
> (Kernberg, 2011, p. 1512)

For love and hate to be creative in a relationship, hate has to be contained by love. Sometimes it isn't.

Violence

Sometimes love and hate manifest in forms of violence. Intimate couple relationships can stir up many primitive intense feelings. For example, loving another can make the self feel very vulnerable, as it breaks through defensive internal structures that have been put in place to protect the self. Intimacy might be longed for but also felt as threatening, engulfing or claustrophobic or as risking betrayal and abandonment. Feelings of exclusion may give rise to jealously, and the otherness of the other may be perceived as abandonment or rejection. It may not be possible to contain these intense feelings in a couple relationship, and hate and aggression, far from being a creative force, become destructive.

While any violence of any kind, emotional and physical, is serious, not all violence is understood in the same way. Joan Kelly and Michael Johnson distinguished between four types of intimate partner violence: coercive controlling violence, violent resistance, situational couple violence and separation instigated violence. Coercive controlling violence is defined as "emotionally abusive intimidation, coercion and control coupled with physical violence used against partners" (Kelly & Johnson, 2008, p. 478), and this usually occurs in the context of other controlling behaviours. Violent resistance is a violent response to coercive controlling violence, and separation instigated violence is a violent response to separation, usually without previous violent behaviour.

As described in Chapter 3, in couple relations the couple projective system can be more developmental or defensive. In situational couple violence, the projections between the partners are often more forceful and excessive. Often an argument between the couple escalates. There may be particular unprocessed elements in the relationship that become triggered and an inability to communicate effectively as heightened feelings take a grip. Julie Humphries and Damian McCann noted that,

> In a heated argument, where there is an attempt to project unbearable feelings into the other, a couple may temporarily

lose the ability to contain feelings, perhaps hitting out in their frustration at not being able to get through to the other.

(Humphries & McCann, 2015, p. 162)

Sometimes it is anger itself that is projected, with one partner carrying the projected anger of the other in addition to his or her own. This has been described as a "double dose" of unprocessed feelings in the projective dynamics of a couple (Pincus, 1962, p. 18; Cleavely, 1993, p. 65). Where there is a fear of one's own anger, that person may need to not only project it into the other but unconsciously or even consciously stimulate it in the other because of the need to seek evidence that it is not part of the self.

Clinical example

The partners in one couple, as I came to understand it, both had a problem with their anger and aggression. On the face of it, it looked like the problem was the wife. When they argued, she could become quite aggressive. But I noticed that when this happened, the husband drew attention to it and, in fact, unconsciously fanned the flames, and so she became even more angry. Then he would point out to me (with some pleasure) how unpleasant she was being and that really there was no point in him saying anything as she didn't listen. It was true that she got angry and couldn't listen. I then felt I had a very polarised couple in front of me – the wife angry and uncontained and the husband becoming increasingly less present and presenting as impotent. The wife found it particularly unbearable that she was being portrayed and perceived in such a negative light. It was only much later in the therapy that the husband felt able to share and acknowledge his own angry feelings towards his wife, which frightened and disturbed him. She had been away on a business trip, and he felt very left by her, a feeling that ran deep in him, resonating with a sense of aloneness he had always felt. His previously vehemently denied anger broke through in this session, and his strength of feeling surprised us all (previously described in Morgan, 2019a, p. 106).

A significant factor in the history of those who use sadistic and controlling violence is the experience of having been victims of violence themselves. As Ruszczynski puts it, "hurt people, hurt people" (Ruszczynski, 2024). Expanding on this comment and drawing on extensive experience of working with violent patients and couples, Ruszczynski states that one way of dealing with the hurt is through projective identification. He argues that acts of violence,

> are often perpetrated by people who feel humiliated, frightened, and vulnerable and, through projective processes and actual behaviour, they rid themselves of these emotions by 'creating' in their victim someone who is at least equally as frightened, or perhaps even more so.
>
> (Ruszczynski, 2012, p. 143)

Lack of containment, mirroring, mentalization and insecure attachment

In sadistic controlling violence, there is a problem with being able to think about and process intensely affective states, including those in the realms of love and hate. This can be understood as resulting from failures occurring in early development, particularly the experience of a lack of containment, or of an absence of contingent mirroring.

In the process of containment as described by Bion, the infant gradually internalises the capacity to process and think about his or her feelings, which Bion called "alpha function". From another perspective, Winnicott described the importance of a mother or primary carer who can accurately mirror the infant's emotional states but in a way that also distinguishes what belongs to the infant and what belongs to her. In both the models of effective containment and mirroring, the infant starts to develop an understanding of his or her own mind and gradually a capacity to think about both his or her mental states and those of others. Ruszczynski argues that in the absence of this the developing person lacks a sense of self that is rooted in the mind; instead, it is rooted in the body.

> Without the experience of containment, no development of a *psychological self* can take place, of a self that can process and

think about experiences and psychic states. Such development requires the primary experience and perception of oneself, *in another person's mind* as thinking and feeling. Without this what results is a 'mindlessness', an empty, inanimate and even malignant sense of self rooted not in the mind but in the body. The incapacity to reflect on and integrate mental experiences results in only the body and bodily experience being available to be used to provide a sense of relief.

(Ruszczynski, 2006, p. 115)

This can be thought about in terms of a failure in the capacity to mentalize. Anthony Bateman and Peter Fonagy describe this concept as follows:

Mentalizing is the process by which we make sense of each other and ourselves, implicitly and explicitly, in terms of subjective states and mental processes. It is a profoundly social phenomenon: as human beings, we generally (and automatically) form beliefs about the mental states of those with whom we interact, and our own mental states are strongly influenced by these beliefs. Nevertheless, human beings can temporarily lose awareness that others have minds, and can even at times treat one another as physical objects.

(Bateman & Fonagy, 2013, p. 595)

Containment, mirroring and mentalization, while describing somewhat different phenomena, all speak to the way in which an individual's psychological self is developed through the mind of another in early development. From this, the capacity to know one's own subjective state, and to be aware of another's subjective state develops. Without this development, it becomes impossible to process one's own mental states, or to be aware of different mental states in another and to have empathy. Mentalization theory is partly rooted in attachment theory (Bowlby, 1969), and those that have studied couple relations from the attachment perspective have found that preoccupied attachment can put the couple at risk of violent interaction. The experience of receiving inconsistent or insensitive care may contribute to developing a preoccupied attachment style in which there is over dependence on others for one's self-esteem and an excessive need for approval from the other. An interpersonal style may develop which is both intrusive and demanding. Kim Bartholomew and colleagues in their review of insecure attachment and intimate partner violence concluded that: "Across studies, and for both genders, pre-occupied attachment was quite consistently associated with both the perpetration of abuse in relationships and the receipt of abuse (or the inclination to return to an abusive relationship)" (Bartholomew et al., 2001, p. 56).

Social and cultural contributors to violent couple relations

The many pressures on the couple from societal and cultural factors that can contribute to intimate partner violence can only briefly be touched upon here. In some societies, women are marginalised and denigrated, and partner violence is culturally sanctioned and therefore accepted.

Internalised homophobia in same sex relationships can lead to self-hatred being directed towards the partner (see Chapter 7). Furthermore, as McCann has pointed out, internalised homo-phobia may cause some sexual minority individuals to feel they are legitimate targets of abuse (McCann, 2024).

Another contemporary concern is the impact of violent porno-graphy on a young person's developing mind and sexuality and the effect this has on their relating. Lemma's review of the research into the impact of violent pornography consumption suggests,

> Sexual coercion, abuse and negative gender attitudes on the part of adolescent boys are significantly associated with con-sumption of online pornography, as is an increased probability of sexting (Stanley et al. 2018a; Ybarra, Mitchell, and Korchmaros, 2011). The impact is not restricted to boys: young girls who use sexually coercive behaviour also report watching violent pornography significantly more than a con-trol group (Kjellgren et al., 2011).
>
> (Lemma, 2021)

Love, hate and the creative couple

Creativity in an intimate relationship does not come from an adherence to romantic love but from an engagement with the whole range of human emotions, from love to hate. In a creative couple relationship, hatred and aggression are present but contained by love. Speaking of mature love and the concern for the other that comes with the depressive position, Ruszczynski writes that in this context, "Aggression may then be recruited in the service of passion and creativity and thus contribute towards the possibility of healthy relationships" (Ruszczynski, 2007, pp. 23–42).

As has been said many times in this book, a fundamental challenge in couple relations is that of encountering the difference and otherness of the other. Being in the presence of otherness is challenging, unsettling and acts as an "interference" negating "the ego's narcissistic confinement in its identity" (Berenstein, 2012), and there is a tendency to extend the boundaries of oneself around the other with whom one is intimately connected. It makes life easier to think the same and agree. However, this is a fundamentally uncreative relationship, as can be seen in mergers like the projective gridlock.

In reality, one comes up against different views – sometimes about important issues – different perceptions, and aspects of the other one can't identify with, doesn't understand or even want to understand. Being angry with the other, not liking or hating something about them is normal. At these times, there can be massive attempts to undo hatred and to find harmony. But often this is by getting into what Bion described as a "-H" state of mind – pushing out of one's mind what is hated in the other or changing it in one's mind into something different and more palatable. However, what is potentially creative, though difficult, is being able to know about and engage with what is hated as well as with what is loved.

Being human means that we have a multitude of feelings under the heading of "love" as well as those under the heading of "hate". If a couple can keep both these aspects alive and contained within a predominantly loving relationship, they will be able to be most alive and creative. The containing capacity of a relationship also increases through surviving the hate and aggression, though clearly in distinction from violence. Mitchell observed that,

> a love that has endured episodic aggression has a depth and resilience obtainable in no other way. Because of love's profound risks, hatred is an inevitable accompaniment, and, paradoxically, the survival of romance depends not on skill in avoiding aggression but on the capacity to contain it alongside love.
>
> (2002, p. 120)

As a relationship matures, engaging with the difference and the otherness of the other, even though sometimes hated, can lead to further knowledge of the other and of the self and to a deepening of love.

Clinical example

One couple came for help because although they felt they had a fundamentally loving relationship they did not feel any sexual desire for each other. They were in their mid-forties, and their youngest child had just started school. Although they had had a good sexual relationship before the children, since having them it had quite quickly fallen away. In one session, they started arguing about going away for the weekend. The husband wanted some grown-up time together without the children, and the wife did not want to leave the children. He became quite insistent, and she became quiet and withdrawn. I felt she really hated him at this point, but I did not think she could properly know that or express it. As he persisted, she became less and less engaged. As the session continued, I felt in touch with split off, hateful feelings between them, and I thought it was this that was killing off any capacity to come together. I eventually commented on the hatred between them, and that although it appeared that she felt he was being cruel and selfish (putting his needs above the children and her), in fact, he also felt she was cruel and selfish by remaining in a clinch with the children which had excluded him while they were infants and continued to do so, when now there was no reason! There was a sense of relief for this couple once I put this into words. I should say that I put this into words that tried to convey that their hatred was real, strong, normal, valid, but containable, I thought, by me initially and, I believed, within their relationship. The couple could then connect with the rage they each felt towards each other, and they brought more feelings; negative feelings about the other that had gone underground, particularly a feeling of utter abandonment by one another during the early child-rearing years. It was clear that these denied feelings had had a profound impact on their sexual feelings about themselves and the other (Morgan, 2019b, p. 19).

Following this exchange between the couple, they were able to be more curious about how the other felt and their own feelings. There was also a process of mourning, of letting go of what had previously been possible in their relationship, when there was just the two of them, but then thinking creatively together about what might need to be re-configured between them in the present. As described earlier, even in the deeper or mature love state, there needs to be a capacity to allow moments of breakdown, to know when one feels pain, disappointment and hatred, to understand misunderstanding and allow one's secure depressive position relationship to come apart and be re-configured in a new way. A creative couple relationship often exists in a place between the paranoid schizoid position and the depressive position. As an old depressive position breaks down, the formation of a new one is, as Britton writes, "not only unknown but unimaginable at this point" (1998, p. 73).

A creative couple bring awareness to what is not working now (even though it might have before), feel secure enough to allow it to come apart, and is confident enough in the relationship to create something new. This happens sometimes in big ways, but more often in small ways many times in a creative couple relationship. In this way, love contains but is also re-found when it is in danger of becoming lost.

George Elliot, in her classic novel *Middlemarch*, said, "Marriage is so unlike anything else. There is something even awful in the nearness it brings" (Cohen, 2021, p. 22). Without the defence of narcissistic illusion or turning a blind eye, the other's "nearness" in an intimate relationship brings the discovery that they are a challenging mixture of things. Cohen suggests the essential paradox of intimacy is, "in intensifying our closeness to another, we not only make them more familiar to us; we come alive to their strangeness and irreducible difference" (2021, p. 23). As they also come alive to ours.

Through the partners becoming able to express their feelings as fully as possible, the other's strangeness and difference can promote curiosity, not only about the other but about the self. "K", or curiosity, helps us be interested in knowing more about both "L" and "H" and less frightened of both. There are many moments in a couple relationship in which ordinary events, some minor, some major, throw the couple into conflict. They come up against difference in the other; sometimes the difference is wanted and valued, and loving feelings take hold. Sometimes it is not, and hateful feelings arise. Struggling with the full range of human feelings gives the relationship life, and being able to do this gives the relationship strength over time.

References

Bartholomew, K., Henderson, A. & Dutton, D. (2001). Insecure attachment and abusive intimate relationships. In: C. Clulow (Ed.), *Sex, Attachment and Couple Psychotherapy: Psychoanalytic Perspectives* (pp. 43–61). London: Karnac.

Bateman, A. & Fonagy, P. (2013). Mentalization-based treatment. *Psychoanalytic Inquiry*, 33: 595–613.

Berenstein, I. (2012). Vínculo as a relationship between others. *Psychoanalytic Quarterly*, 81 (3): 565–577.

Bion, W. R. (1962). *Learning from Experience*. London: Karnac.

Bott Spillius, E., Milton, J., Garvey, P., Couve, C. & Steiner, D. (2011). *The New Dictionary of Kleinian Thought*. London & New York: Routledge.

Bowlby, J. (1969). *Attachment and Loss: Volume I: Attachment*. The International Psycho-Analytical Library, Vol. 79 (pp. 1–401). London: Hogarth Press and the Institute of Psycho-Analysis.

Britton, R. (1998). Before and after the depressive position Ps (n)→D (n)→Ps (n +1). In: R. Britton, *Belief and Imagination: Explorations in Psychoanalysis* (pp. 69–81). London: Routledge.

Cleavely, E. (1993). Relationships: Interaction, defences, and transformation. In: S. Ruszczynski (Ed.), *Psychotherapy with Couples: Theory and*

Practice at the Tavistock Institute of Marital Studies (pp. 55–69). London: Karnac.

Cohen, J. (2021). *The Guardian Review*, Sunday March 2021, issue no. 165.

Fisher, J. (1999). *The Uninvited Guest: Emerging from Narcissism towards Marriage*. London: Karnac.

Freud, S. (1905). *Three Essays on the Theory of Sexuality (1905)*. In: The Standard Edition of the Complete Psychological Works of Sigmund Freud, Volume 7: A Case of Hysteria, Three Essays on Sexuality and Other Works (1901–1905) (pp. 123–246). London: Hogarth Press.

Freud, S. (1913). *Totem and Taboo: Some Points of Agreement between the Mental Lives of Savages and Neurotics (1913 [1912–13])*. In: The Standard Edition of the Complete Psychological Works of Sigmund Freud, Volume 13: Totem and Taboo and Other Works (1913–1914) (pp. vii–162). London: Hogarth Press.

Freud, S. (1915). *Instincts and their Vicissitudes*. In: The Standard Edition of the Complete Psychological Works of Sigmund Freud, Volume 14: On the History of the Psycho-Analytic Movement, Papers on Metapsychology and Other Works (pp. 109–140). London: Hogarth Press.

Friend, J. (2013). Love as a creative illusion and its place in psychoanalytic couple psychotherapy. *Couple and Family Psychoanalysis*, 3 (1): 3–14.

Friend, J. (2021). Creative illusion in couples: Thoughts about the value of transitional experience for couple relationships. *Couple and Family Psychoanalysis*, 11 (2): 158–169. London: Phoenix.

Grier, F. (2009). Lively and deathly intercourse. In C. Clulow (Ed.), *Sex, Attachment and Couple Psychotherapy: Psychoanalytic Perspectives* (pp. 45–61). London: Karnac.

Hewison, D. (2023). Re-visioning creativity in couple psychanalysis: The importance of Winnicott and Bollas in clinical practice. In: S. Nathans (Ed.), *More about Couples on the Couch: Approaching Psychoanalytic Couple Psychotherapy from an Expanded Perspective*. London & New York: Routledge.

Humphries, J. & McCann, D. (2015). Couple psychoanalytic psychotherapy with violent couples: Understanding and working with domestic violence. *Couple and Family Psychoanalysis*, 5 (2): 149–167.

Joyce, A. (2019). The couple, the self, and the problem of the other. *Couple and Family Psychoanalysis*, 6 (2): 181–193.

Kelly, J. B. & Johnson, M. P. (2008). Differentiation among types of intimate partner violence: Research update and implications for interventions. *Family Court Review*, 46 (3): 476–499.

Kernberg, O. F. (1995). *Love Relations: Normality and Pathology*. New Haven: Yale University Press.

Kernberg, O. F. (2011). Limitations to the capacity to love. *International Journal of Psychoanalysis*, 92: 1501–1515.

Kirson-Trilling, O. (2022). The binds that bond: Disavowed vulnerability in couples with early relational trauma. *Couple and Family Psychoanalysis*, 12 (2).

Lemma, A. (2021). Introduction – Becoming sexual in digital times: The risks and harms of online pornography. *The Psychoanalytic Study of the Child*, 74(1): 118–130.

McCann, D. (2024). Understanding the nature and impact of sexual violence and abuse in the lives of lesbians, gay men, bisexuals and transgender individuals and couples. *Couple and Family Psychoanalysis*, 14(1).

Mitchell, S. (2002). *Can Love last?: The Fate of Romance over Time*. New York & London: W.W. Norton & Company.

Morgan, M. (1995). The projective gridlock: A form of projective identification in couple relationships. In: S. Ruszczynski & J. V. Fisher (Eds.), *Intrusiveness and Intimacy in the Couple* (pp. 33–48). London: Karnac.

Morgan, M. (2019a). *A Couple State of Mind: Psychoanalysis of Couples and the Tavistock Relationships Model*. London & New York: Routledge.

Morgan, M. (2019b). Love, hate, and otherness in intimate relating. *Couple and Family Psychoanalysis*, 9: 15–21.

Novakovic, A. (2016). The quarrelling couple. In: A. Novakovic (Ed.), *Couple Dynamics: Psychoanalytic Perspectives in Work with the Individual, the Couple and the Group* (pp. 85–105). London: Karnac.

Person, E. S. (1988). *Dreams of Love and Fateful Encounters: The Power of Romantic Passion*. New York: W.W. Norton.

Pickering, J. (2008). *Being in Love: Therapeutic Pathways through Psychological Obstacles to Love*. London & New York: Routledge.

Pincus, L. (1962). The nature of marital interaction. In: The Institute of Marital Studies (Ed.), *The Marital Relationship as a Focus for Casework* (pp. 13–25). London: Institute of Marital Studies.

Ruszczynski, S. (2006). Sado-masochistic enactments in a couple relationship: the fear of intimacy and the dread of separateness. *Psychoanalytic Perspectives on Couple Work*, (2): 107–116.

Ruszczynski, S. (2007). The problem of certain psychic realities: Aggression and violence as perverse solutions. In: D. Morgan & S. Ruszczynski (Eds.), *Lectures on Violence, Perversion and Delinquency* (pp. 23–42). London: Routledge.

Ruszczynski, S. (2012). Personality disorder: A diagnosis of disordered relating. *Couple and Family Psychoanalysis*, 2: 133–148.

Ruszczynski, S. (2024). Personal communication.

Steiner, J. (2017). Melanie Klein's technique then and now. Institute of Psychoanalysis UK Audio Video Project 1:15.

Steiner, J. (2024). Differentiating between romantic and mature love: Revisiting the three caskets. *The International Journal of Psychoanalysis*, 105: 564–575.

Index

For Product Safety Concerns and Information please contact our EU
representative GPSR@taylorandfrancis.com
Taylor & Francis Verlag GmbH, Kaufingerstraße 24, 80331 München, Germany

www.ingramcontent.com/pod-product-compliance
Lightning Source LLC
Chambersburg PA
CBHW071746270326
41928CB00013B/2820